The Fox Herder's Guide

How to Lead Teams
That Inform and Motivate
Organizational Change

by

Earl Boebert

Illustrated
by
Russell Boebert

ISBN-10: 978-0-9836506-1-4

"It's pretty easy, but it's pretty hard"
—Dainin Katagiri Roshi

To Absent Friends:

Jim Anderson
Ted Glaser
Paul Kargcr
Bob Morris
Rick Proto
Howard Rosenblum
Milt Zaslow

Contents

Foreword   1

Hedgehogs, Foxes, and You   7

Beginner's Mind   15

Be Of Two Minds   21

Work At It   31

Teams   35

Resource Planning   51

Troubling Thoughts   65

Task Planning   75

Early Days   93

Factoids Into Findings   99

Getting To Recommendations   113

Getting The Word Out   133

Afterword   158

Postscript   159

Notes   160

THE
FOX HERDER'S
GUIDE

The law of Perseverance
is one of the deepest in man:
by nature he hates change;
seldom will he quit his old house
till it has actually fallen about his ears.
—Thomas Carlyle[1]

Foreword

History is littered with the bones of organizations killed by change, either because they let events run over them, or because they misjudged what was happening to them. When you look closely at those organizations that have changed successfully, it is often clear that somewhere, somehow, somebody did their homework. That's the subject of this book: how to do your homework in a way that both motivates and informs rational organizational change.

I've done a lot of such homework in the course of almost a half-century of technical work, and intend to pass on what I've learned to those of you who may just be starting. In this book I explore the causes of both success and failure in motivating rational change. I cover two broad topics: the attributes of mind and character which lead you to the discovery of truth, and the mechanics of using that knowledge to influence others. The first is analogous to artistic ability, the second is analogous to a grasp of artistic technique. Ability without technique leads to works that are powerful but crude; technique without ability leads to works that are slick but shallow. It takes both ability and technique to create a masterpiece; it takes proper attributes of mind as well as a grasp of planning, management and communication techniques to perform a study that will make a difference.

My definition of "studies" ranges from informal undertakings by small groups to the highly structured policy studies of organizations like the National Academy of Sciences, and spans efforts such as business plans, technical proposals, incident investigations and security studies. The common theme of all studies is that they seek the truth, use facts to convince, and are large and complex enough to require a team.

Foreword

Although I address my remarks mainly to team leaders, you will find much of value if you are a member of a study team, someone who is presented with a study and wants to see what should go into a successful one, or just an ordinary soul who wants to get to the bottom of some matter or another.

I learned these lessons a while ago, and fully understand that "the past is a foreign country: they do things differently there."[2] But human nature stays much the same, and it's the human aspect of these efforts which is my focus.

I hope this guide will lead you into the world of seeking the truth and doing the right thing. Your efforts may not lead to either wealth or fame, but you'll probably make solid friendships during the process. You might even join those lucky few who can look back at some time in their lives and say: "it was important, we got it right, and it made a difference."

Basics

Hedgehogs,
Foxes,
and
You

> *The fox knows many little things,*
> *but the hedgehog knows one big thing.*
> *—Archilocus[3]*

The line of ancient Greek poetry at the top of this page remained the exclusive concern of classical scholars until 1953, when the philosopher Isaiah Berlin published an essay called "The Hedgehog and the Fox." In it he used Archilochus' imagery to illustrate a division of intellectuals into two categories: hedgehogs and foxes. Hedgehogs

> *relate everything to a single central vision, one system, more or less coherent and articulate, in terms of which they understand, think, and feel...*

while foxes

> *pursue many ends, often unrelated and even contradictory ... related by no moral or aesthetic principal.*

Berlin listed Plato, Nietzsche, and Pascal as hedgehogs and Shakespeare, Montaigne and Aristotle as foxes. He then turned his attention to the true subject of the essay, which was how Tolstoy viewed the writing of history.[4]

Calling people hedgehogs and foxes is immensely popular; a Google search will turn up over a million references to the words. Much of this popularity, at least to the current generation, is due to a book on corporate management by the researcher and educator James C. Collins.[5] In it he presents the common knowledge that the "one big thing" the hedgehog knows is how to defeat the attacks of the fox by rolling up into a ball and becoming:

> ... *a sphere of sharp spikes ... The fox ... sees the hedgehog defense and calls off the attack. ... Each day, some version of this battle between the hedgehog and the fox takes place, and despite the greater cunning of the fox, the hedgehog always wins.*

This interpretation of Archilocus' enigmatic phrase is then used to introduce a way of thinking, which involves reducing

9

all challenges and dilemmas to simple — indeed almost simplistic — hedgehog ideas. For a hedgehog, anything that does not somehow relate to the hedgehog ideas holds no relevance.

He goes to argue that managing according to this "Hedgehog Concept" will enable a corporate leader to achieve greatness.

A second boost to the spread of the metaphor was given by the psychologist Philip Tetlock in an extended study of political forecasters,[6] whom he divides into hedgehogs and foxes in this way:

The metaphorical meaning oscillates over time, but it never strays far from eclectic cunning (foxes) and dogged persistence (hedgehogs). [7]

He then goes on to argue that the foxes do better in forecasting than the hedgehogs, but the hedgehogs are more effective in the media because of their forceful exposition of a single world view.

So far, so good. Berlin gets a "narrative hook" to start his essay on Tolstoy. Collins, Tetlock and I can put ourselves in the company of a major intellect of the 20th century, and I get a title and a nice cover illustration. All very satisfactory, until you start digging.

Start with Archilocus. He was, as far as we can know for someone who lived 2600 years ago, an interesting character: poet, wanderer, mercenary soldier and satirist.[8] His line of poetry about hedgehogs and foxes is only seven words long in the original Greek, and was found by itself on a scrap of parchment. Which raises the question: what if there had been a second line that read "and that one big thing is wrong?"

That's not as farfetched as it might seem, given the earthy barracks humor that Archilochus exhibits in other surviving fragments.[9] He also probably spent a lot of time in the field, where he may have actually seen foxes go at hedgehogs and learned that, contrary to the common knowledge quoted above, the fox often wins.[10] It is also plausible that a professional soldier would be unimpressed by a stratagem that cedes both full mobility and the initiative to your adversary — in fact, a classicist whom Berlin asked about the quote[11] had argued previously that Archilochus identified with the fox.[12]

And then there is the enigmatic nature of the words themselves. In response to a critique of Berlin's use of the metaphor, at least one set of experts said:

Thus, we fear the most that can be said about the Archilochean fragment is that there is no one transparently correct interpretation of it—only many different risky ones. [13]

Berlin himself was careful to point out the limits of his metaphor, first in the essay itself:

Of course, like all over-simple classifications of this type, the dichotomy becomes, if pressed, artificial, scholastic and ultimately absurd. [14]

And again, in the exchange of letters referenced above:

I used [Archilochus'] isolated line as a peg on which to hang my own reflections: the metaphor of hedgehogs and foxes was not, I warned the reader, to be driven too far; it was intended, at most, as an opening to my central theme—a hypothesis about the psychological roots of Tolstoy's historical outlook. Still less did I mean to imply that foxes were superior to hedgehogs; this was (and is) not my view. I made no judgments of value. [15]

The labels were simply to be

a point of view from which to look and compare, a starting-point for genuine investigation. [16]

In other words, move along folks, you've learned all there is to learn from this metaphor.

Things get even dicier when we move to the next level: authors alluding to Berlin alluding to what Archilochus may or may not have meant. Collins moves from the arena of retrospective analysis to prospective decision-making, and assigns to his metaphorical hedgehog a tactical superiority not exhibited by the real ones. Tetlock has the problem that the metaphor is binary but the world is analog; one could hardly justify saying that either Shakespeare or Montaigne lacked perseverance, and when Tetlock gets into details he is forced to consider fox-hedgehog and hedgehog-fox hybrids, people who presumably know both one big thing and many small ones at the same time. For me, the metaphor simply provides a superficial illustration of title and book cover, and a deeper illustration that something you think you understand may not survive closer scrutiny.

At this point you're probably thinking "well, he certainly beat that topic to death." Precisely. Beating topics to death and staying close to the facts is the way you get it right. To stay close to to the facts you must first obtain them, like my favorite amphibian.

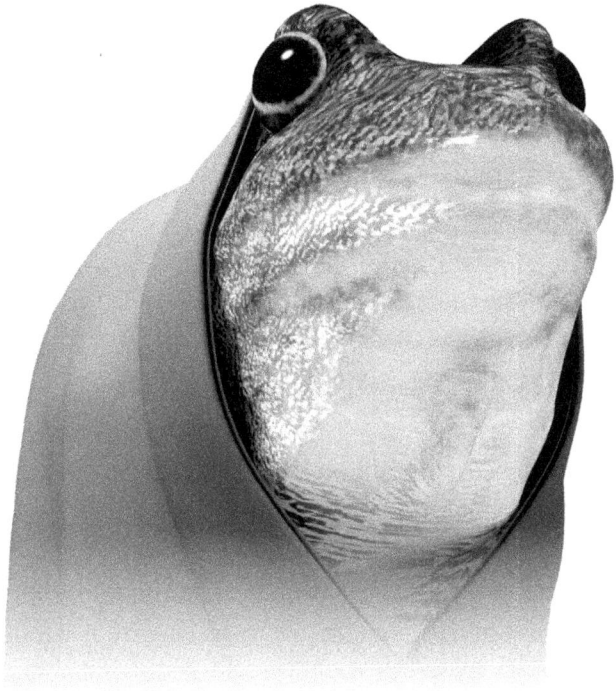

Beginner's Mind

15

You should be like a frog always.
—Shunryu Suzuki Roshi [17]

Consider the frog. It sits on its lily pad, eyes wide open, a model of pure observation. A fly buzzes within range of that tongue and zap! Lunch.

This is what Suzuki Roshi meant when he said you should be like a frog. It was his way of illustrating "Beginner's Mind," the ability to pay attention the way you did when you were a child and everything you saw was so new and impressive that it occupied your whole consciousness. It is what psychologists call "mindfulness."

Beginner's Mind captures reality the way the frog captures a fly: immediately, reflexively, without conscious thought, in a single aha! moment. It's what I think was operating when a humble clerk captured the reality of something that wasn't there, and went on to topple a king's empire.

16

The King and the Clerk

In the late 1890s, King Leopold II of Belgium owned a colony in Africa. The colony, called the Congo Free State, was not a government entity but rather the personal property of Leopold. He strictly controlled access to it, promoted it to the world as a humanitarian activity, and grew rich on the profits. Contrary to Leopold's propaganda, the colony was a place so horrific it served as the inspiration for Conrad's *Heart of Darkness*. [18]

Things were going swimmingly for Leopold until the arc of his life crossed that of a young Englishman by the name of Edmund Dene Morel. At first glance, E.D. Morel didn't look like much of a potential threat to Leopold II, King of the Belgians, President of the Congo Free State and one of the wealthiest men on the planet. In fact, at first glance E.D. Morel didn't look like much of anything at all. The son of an Englishwoman and a minor French bureaucrat who died early and left her without a pension, Morel quit school at fifteen to support his mother and finally ended up as a clerk in a shipping company. You could easily see someone like him scratching away at a desk all day, then maybe a pint or two at the pub and home to dear old mum — and doing it all over again tomorrow. Just another timeclock puncher in the vast commercial hive that was Victorian Liverpool. But it didn't turn out that way at all.

Morel's company did all the shipping for the Congo Free State, and because he was fluent in French, he became his employer's liaison to the Brussels offices of the colony. In the course of doing this, Morel noted what was being shipped in to the colony, which was mainly arms and ammunition, and what was being shipped out, which was ivory and rubber. Most importantly, Morel noted what was *not* being shipped to Africa: foodstuffs and other goods that would serve to compensate the residents of the colony for their labors. Morel accurately concluded that Leopold was running a slave state. In addition, he discovered substantial differences between the amount of ivory and rubber that his company was shipping and the amounts the colony was reporting to the public in support of their carefully constructed "humanitarian" image. Not only was it a slave state, somebody was skimming. The whole structure presented by Leopold to the world was a lie.

With a level of energy that was remarkable even by Victorian standards, Morel began a campaign of public exposure during which he wrote books and innumerable letters, founded a newspaper, and enlisted the support of people like Sir Arthur Conan Doyle, Mark Twain, and the Archbishop of Canterbury. In 1908 Leopold lost control of his colony, but the damage he did to its people lasts to this day.[19] And it all started with Beginner's Mind, grasping that which wasn't there.

Getting There

Some people are born with Beginner's Mind, and never lose it; others, like myself, have had to work at it. A proven method for doing so is the practice of meditation. Today meditation practice has achieved legitimacy, mainly as a consequence of advances in the study of brain function,[20] but thirty years ago it was something fairly unusual for a hard core techie like myself to undertake.

There are a variety of traditions in which to learn how to meditate, each with its own secular or spiritual basis. I happened to study Zen under Dainin Katagiri Roshi[21] in Minneapolis, but that was just an accident of time and place. There are plenty of routes to the same mental capacity.[22]

And it's not enough just to grasp reality, you have to do something about it. Morel didn't just sit there with a self-satisfied smile when he made his discovery: he wrote, and wrote, and wrote some more. Which brings up the topic of words.

Be Of Two Minds

In the Zen way of looking at the world, everything has two aspects, Phenomenal and Essential. The Phenomenal is what we perceive and can put into words, the Essential is the true nature of the object. The Phenomenal is what Mumon means by the term "words;" the Essential is what he means by the term "no-words." His point is that you have to use both, simultaneously, and you can't sit around dreaming about it: being alive requires that you act every instant, if only to breathe.

People like Mumon devised paradoxical riddles called "koans" to lock up your mind and force you to break out of the realm of words. They broke sticks and kicked over water jugs to demonstrate that there's more to sticks, and water jugs, and everything else than can be be expressed in mere words.

Whether you accept Mumon's world view or not, it is important that you appreciate the general Zen teaching that you must tightly control the language-processing part of your mind. This is your "Categorizing Mind," one that constantly tries to substitute its structures of labels and categories for the facts that are staring you in the face. If you let it get away with that, the consequences can be dire.

Fatal Logic

The German defeat in World War II was hastened because they protected most of their radio communications using a cipher machine called Enigma, whose coding system was broken by Allied cryptanalysts. That effort, eventually called ULTRA, began with a theoretical breakthrough by the Poles before the war,[24] continued with the brilliant work of Alan Turing at Bletchley Park in England,[25] and finished up with industrial-scale mechanical decryption at Bletchley and Washington, D.C.[26]

It was crucial that the Germans not discover that the Allies were, in effect, reading their minds. Yet throughout the war, whenever the Germans questioned whether their communications security had been compromised, they relied on their own internal analysis of their own machine, and over and over again concluded that a breach was mathematically unlikely to the point of impossibility. This was particularly true late in the war, when the German submarine fleet was suffering losses of such a magnitude that it was obvious that something had to be going on.

One historian, a mathematician, described it this way:

Bletchley's continued successes depended upon the willingness of German authorities to believe that ciphers were proved *secure, instead of asking whether they actually were. It was a military Gödel theorem, in which systematic inertia rendered the German leadership incapable of looking at their system from the outside.*[27]

The language that trapped them was mathematics instead of German or English, but the effect was the same: a structure internal to their minds trumped external reality.

And that's not the worst thing Categorizing Mind can do to you. Categories lead to generalization, and generalization can lead to gross error.

All Ruritarians

Let's say you have occasion to come in contact with members of an ethnic and cultural group which I'll call "Ruritanians." True to their name, all the Ruritanians you encounter seem not to be very intelligent and do many silly things. Your Categorizing Mind then kicks in and you generate a label with attributes: "All Ruritanians are buffoons."

Then you come down from the general to the specific when encountering a Ruritanian named Vladimir. "All Ruritanians are buffoons. Vladimir is a Ruritanian. Therefore Vladimir is a buffoon." Much mischief has devolved from such constructs, often by individuals eager to fool themselves or others.

When you think, say, or write that Vladimir "is" a buffoon, you confuse the label in your Categorizing Mind with Vladimir's essential nature. Unless you have seen him function in every possible circumstance you really don't know what his essential nature is.

On the other hand, if you replaced the label with the more precise and less generalizing observation "Vladimir acts like a buffoon," you open many other possibilities: Vladimir may be educable, he may be acting that way for a reason, or he may act like a buffoon only under certain circumstances.

Replacing the verb "to be" with a careful description is a way of avoiding Categorizing Mind. Writing this way even has a name and formal rules: it is called "English Prime" or "E-Prime."[28] Use these rules with care lest they become just another trap set by your Categorizing Mind.

If a counterexample to some description is encountered, you shouldn't reflexively discard that description. Rather, you should consider the alternative that the description may be "almost right." The concept of "almost right" approximates Imre Lakatos' notion that mathematical proofs are done not to produce a compelling argument, but rather to refine the theorem under scrutiny. Each time a proof is refuted, the theorem in question is made more exact.[29] Isaac Asimov called this "The Relativity of Wrong."[30]

Now look again at our friend Vladimir. You begin with the label "Vladimir is a buffoon." Then you obtain evidence of Vladimir acting intelligently. If you stick with your Categorizing Mind, you have an

27

apparent contradiction: Vladimir simultaneously is and is not a buffoon.

If, on the other hand, you start out with "Vladimir acts like a buffoon," the new evidence sharpens this by adding a condition: "Vladimir acts like a buffoon under certain circumstances; at other times he acts quite intelligently." Now you have something to investigate: under what circumstances does Vladimir act like a buffoon? Digging into this may reveal that his behavior is a ruse to divert attention while an accomplice picks someone's pocket. Now you have a further refinement: "Vladimir acts in a simpleminded fashion immediately prior to pickpocketing attempts; at other times he acts intelligently." If you had stayed inside your categorizing mind you might have lost your wallet.

Kathryn Schultz has written an excellent study of what she calls "wrongology," the human predilection for making and holding on to mistakes.[31] When reading it (which you should definitely do), observe the number of times the errors she describes result from letting Categorizing Mind take over the perception of reality.

Use Both Minds

The trick, then is to use each mind when appropriate, and avoid getting trapped in either. Use Beginner's Mind to see essential reality, but don't get drunk on insights. Use Categorizing Mind to communicate, but always remember that any structure made of language has the potential to trap you inside itself.

Work At It

At first mountains are mountains.
Then they aren't mountains.
Finally they are mountains again.
—Old Zen Saying[32]

A Zen sesshin is an event where students live like monks for several days, meditating all day with minimal breaks for meals and exercise, and speaking as little as possible. It includes short private sessions with the Roshi.

I was having a very hard time at one of my first sesshins. It had been difficult for me to decide to attend and even more difficult for me to fit it into my schedule, so I began with high expectations. As I proceeded my mind fought the meditation process and my body was tensing up to the point I was in almost constant pain. I explained this to Katagiri Roshi and told him that as a middle-aged guy with stiff muscles I didn't know if I could stick it out to the end. "Ah," he said, "you are ready to begin." And so I began, and eventually got through it. What he got across to me was that the acquisition of insight is not a spectator sport.

This understanding is captured in the three essentials of Zen practice: *dai-shinkon,* Great Faith, *dai-gidan,* Great Doubt, and *dai-funshin*, Great Perseverance.[33]

Great Faith means you have to operate on faith as you strive toward a goal, because you're not there yet; in fact, you're not sure there's even a there, there.

Great doubt is that point where you hit rock bottom, and think you can't possibly go any further. This is the point where find yourself totally bewildered. This is actually good, because it indicates you are confronted with a hard problem, and hard problems yield important results.

Great Perseverance means you keep at it, through the Great Doubt. The most important thing is to start, anywhere: "No cryptogram was ever solved by staring at it."[34] Generate a hypothesis, any hypothesis, and apply it. It won't be right, but you'll learn something. "Ever failed. No matter. Try again. Fail again. Fail better."[35] You know when you're operating on Great

Perseverance when you can say: "It was the first thing I thought of when I awakened, the last when I fell asleep."[36]

This level of effort is more necessary than ever in an era when quick answers can be had for the expenditure of a few keystrokes in a Web search or a question dispatched to Twitter. An important study requires much more than you'll find in a Wikipedia article.

Get ready for a long hard grind of wading through false positives; if you grew up with the pushbutton answers of the Internet it may be the longest and hardest you've experienced so far, and require that you learn to focus in a way not taught by hopping from Twitter to email to text message on your telephone.

All attributes of mind and character I've described so far have to do with you as an individual. The next section deals with teams, objectives, process, and leadership.

Teams

Happy families are all alike;
every unhappy family is unhappy in its own way.
—Leo Tolstoy[37]

The position of cook, or Tenzo, is a very important one in a traditional Zen monastery; in some places, it was the last job a monk has before becoming Roshi. Being Tenzo was good training for being Roshi because traditional Zen was a mendicant order, which is to say that the monks begged for their food in addition to raising some, if space permitted. So the Tenzo had to improvise meals — whatever rolled in that day was dinner. With the Roshi, whoever showed up at the door wanting to learn was your student.[38] And you may find similarly that your team is picked for you.

The attitude of the Tenzo and Roshi is a good one to adopt. I've been on, and led, a fair number of teams, and the more experience I have the less weight I put on judging people's potential usefulness before I see them work in the team environment. I've had individuals that were literally dumped into my lap as a way of getting rid of them blossom into major contributors, and people who have come with impressive resumes turn into total duds or, more commonly, be so disruptive to team activities that I had to give them the boot.

I think the reason for this has to do with team dynamics and the fact that for most of us, our ability to perform is very context-dependent. So my advice is that within broad boundaries of previous experience, you just never can tell, and all you can do is roll the dice and react to whatever numbers come up — with one exception. These are the individuals who are way over on the hedgehog end of the spectrum, armed with a unitary internal vision they inherited from someone else. They embody Emerson's remark that

> *A foolish consistency is the hobgoblin of little minds, adored by little statesmen and philosophers and divines.* [39]

You'll run into them most frequently in studies dealing with public policy, although adherents to various philosophies of science and software development methodologies can be just as bad. They are walking examples of Nietzsche's aphorism that

Convictions are more dangerous enemies of truth than lies.[40]

I confess that I will stoop to, or excuse, practically any level of Machiavellian behavior required to get rid of one of these people.[41]

Similarly, people who are "all fox" are often worthless because they'll flit from topic to topic without digging deep enough into any one of them to generate useful results. So if you have the ability to select members of your team, look for people who are nimble foxes when it comes to capturing and weighing evidence but steady hedgehogs when it comes to matters of character, such as determination and loyalty to the truth.

Your Skulk of Foxes

It has been my experience that Tolstoy's observation about families applies to teams working on intangibles like studies and software: the successful ones proceed in pretty much the same fashion and the unsuccessful ones keep inventing new ways to fail. I am likewise convinced that all successful teams share three characteristics: clear objectives, a defined process, and effective leadership. I will discuss each in turn.

Clear Objectives

The studies we're concerned with will have both a strategic and a tactical objective. The strategic objective is rational change on the part of some institution. It will be vague in the beginning ("We have to do something about X") and become more specific as the study proceeds. Your tactical objective is something you produce to achieve your strategic objective, and is almost always some kind of narrative.

These narratives send a common message: "this is the situation and this is what we should do about it." They differ from historical treatises in that they contain calls for action; they differ from political propaganda in that the calls for action are supported by fact and reason instead of fear, bigotry, or superstition.

The form of your narrative will vary according to the technology of your time and the culture of your institution. Some of these narratives will have to convey your message all by themselves: things like paper reports, e-books, Web pages, podcasts, or videos. Others may be delivered "live" and in an interactive fashion, such as in a briefing or a seminar.

What's constant across the forms is the need for you to convey complex and subtle insights to an audience accustomed to tweets, three-minute YouTube videos, and talking points delivered by talking heads on cable news. What varies are the stratagems you use to get your message across.

Whatever the form, the critical content of your narrative will be findings and recommendations. Findings are statements of fact, backed by evidence: "this is the situation." Recommendations are actions that should be taken, and they in turn are supported by the findings: "this is what should be done about it." Everything else is background.

Defined Process

Inventing your process as you go along almost always results in inventing a new way to fail. The process I outline below is one I have used over and over with success. It is built on the principles that there is only so much that the human mind can absorb at a time, that the development of insights is an evolutionary process in which large conclusions are synthesized from small beginning elements, and that you have to input energy to get there; it won't happen by itself.

The beginning elements I call "factoids" and "issues." A factoid is the seed of of a finding, and an issue is the seed of a recommendation. Factoids are things that patent attorneys refer to as being "in the air," that is, surmises which are part of, or can be readily drawn from, the current state of knowledge. As each factoid is captured it must be analyzed and refined, or deemed as hopelessly untrue and discarded. As each issue is conceived it must be expanded to include the possible positions that can be taken with regard to it, and those positions tied to the factoids that support them.

Factoids evolve into findings as they are reviewed and evaluated by the team. This activity resembles the various collaborative efforts that occur on the Internet, such as when a question is asked on a specialist forum and various knowledgeable contributors interact to come up with a refined answer.

Recommendations require more structure, and it is important that your team understand and agree to the process by which they are to be arrived at. The issues are first organized into a decision tree, and then the team "prunes" the tree by selecting some positions and rejecting others. This is the time when you will exercise your leadership skills to guide a true consensus that converges to a result.

Once the team shares a common understanding of what should be done and why, this understanding is then embodied in the appropriate narrative or narratives.

Effective Leadership

There are two broad divisions in Zen, known as Rinzai and Soto. Rinzai ("The Warrior") is more energetic and Soto ("The Farmer") is more patient. Both Rinzai and Soto monasteries are supervised by Roshis, but the style of leadership is much different. Using the sword as a metaphor for authority, an old saying is that in Rinzai Zen the sword is waved under your nose, while in Soto Zen it remains sheathed on the Roshi's desk. But it's always there.

The Rinzai approach works when you are in charge of an activity where you can see what everybody is doing and are able to give orders like a construction foreman.

Studies aren't like that: team members may be at distant locations, and even if you can watch what they are up to, all you'll see most of the time is somebody staring at a computer display. You can't tell if they're doing good work, bad work, or no work at all. They're working on what Fred Brooks famously called "thought-stuff,"[42] a product which is at once intangible and important. Now you must motivate individuals to work independently toward a common goal. This requires the Soto approach: you exercise your authority when you have to, but not before; up to that point you lead by respect.

Authority is granted by your position in an organization, but respect is earned: it is the feeling of trust and confidence you inspire in others. Along with your skills and knowledge, the ability to command respect is a form of personal power that stays with you whatever job you hold. The power granted by some organization, on the other hand, is situational and ephemeral. Today you may be the Vice President of Everything; but tomorrow you could be just another sad case in the unemployment line.[43]

When you are dealing with a team of volunteers, you have minimal formal authority — about all you can do is ask somebody to leave. Even when you are conducting the study inside a formal structure such as a corporation, you will find that in today's world you have much less formal authority than you might think. Pensions are portable, health benefits are often minimal, and the inhibitions against walking out the door, especially for the good people, are much less than they used to be. In a sense everybody has become a freelancer. So the wisest course is to treat everyone as a volunteer, and seek to gain, rather than coerce, effort and cooperation.

The best way I know how to go about this is what I call "guided consensus," captured in the remark "there go my people; I must get in front of them, for I am their leader."[44]

This doesn't mean you're a doormat; quite the opposite. It means you are uncompromising when it comes to quality of work, maintaining the objective, staying within your resources, and making your schedule. Within those limits, you let the team pretty much run itself.

Leadership is exercised by example; what you say is largely irrelevant, what you do is critical. If you show up a half-hour late for a meeting and deliver a lecture on schedule discipline, everybody will get the message — just not the one you intended. If your team has to work late, you show up as well, if only to do the midnight McDonald's run. If there are financial incentives, such as in a product plan or a proposal, make sure they are shared among the team members. These are the actions that make the difference between a cohesive team and a Dilbertian dystopia.[45]

The final, and in my view most essential, aspect of leadership has to do with responsibility, as exemplified by Dwight Eisenhower, who during the early hours of the D-Day invasion carried a note which he had drafted to be released in case the landings failed. The last line was: "If any blame or fault attaches to the attempt it is mine alone."[46]

Everyone under him knew from his actions and demeanor that he bore the burdens of both authority and responsibility.[47] On the other hand, if the person supposedly in charge makes it clear by their actions and demeanor that they will own the victories and the rest of the team will own the defeats, then team cohesion will probably never come about — except perhaps as a revolt against that person.

Plan
Your
Work

Resource
Planning

*When everybody is busy stuffing food in the freezer, it's your
job to make sure it's plugged into the wall.*
—*J.J. Renier* [48]

Before you can lay out a task plan, you have to know what resources you'll have. Before you can think about resources, you have to know something about the scope of your study.

When thinking about scope you need to consider both the internals and the externals of your effort. The externals are obvious: the strategic objective, the deadlines, and the budget. The internals are your forecast of how the study will unfold: The size and makeup of the team, whether members will be located in one place or geographically dispersed, and where the factoids are going to come from: the Internet, interviews, briefings, field trips, whatever.

Once you've thought about those things, you can then move on to the resource questions: the size and makeup of the team, the physical nature of the study file of factoids and issues, and how the team is going to communicate with the study file and each other. All these elements of scope influence your estimates of time and money, which will then constrain what kind of task plan you can devise.

Sometimes you plan from objectives to resources: "What would it take to figure out X?" Other times you get the resources first: "Here's what we've got, how much study of X will that let us do?" Most generally it's a kind of negotiation, where you go back and forth between resources and objectives. In all cases it's essential to sort this out before you start, so you don't find yourself in over your head after you've promised a result.

There's not much to be said about time and money in a book of general advice such as this, except for one thing: if you have a chance to choose between longer schedule or more money, opt for the longer schedule. "Think time" is the most precious resource when working with "thought-stuff."

Objectives

If your objectives are given by some defining document, such as a statement of work, selection criteria, or regulation, your first step should be to make an annotated version in which you map each term and phrase into the terminology of your endeavor. If at all possible, you should review your annotated version with the relevant authorities, in order to avoid expensive misunderstandings down the road.

In the course of doing this you will quite probably discover holes, redundancies, and inconsistencies in the governing document. In extreme cases these may cause you to question the wisdom of proceeding. The annotated version will be a powerful tool to get your concerns across to others. If you decide to go ahead, the annotated version will efficiently get your team started.

If you're not given a defining document then you have to write your own to insure that the study objectives are clearly stated and to help keep them stable. You should also be alert to the fact that members of the team may have their own ideas of what the objectives should be, and you need to know how much flexibility you have in resetting them. If the answer is "not much," you have to figure out how you explain that fact to the team in a way that maintains team cohesion and motivation.

The Study File

Back in the day, we did all this with 3 x 5 cards and strips of paper thumbtacked to the walls of the "boiler room" where the team camped out. Now there are software tools which make things easier, and also enable work to be done by geographically distributed teams.

The central tool for driving progress is the study file where the team maintains the issues and factoids. This is a good place to use a "Wiki,"[49] which is a collaboratively generated and maintained on-line document.

No tool, whether card file or Wiki, will think for you, but it will capture thoughts that people have had. In particular, the linking capabilities of the Wiki enable issues to be tied to the factoids that support them, and factoids tied to references, text, or multimedia that support their veracity.

Each element of the file will be a block of text. Issues will have the structure "this is something we must decide and these are the options;" factoids will say "this is what we know and this is why we know it." Later in the endeavor, as the team generates findings and recommendations, the residue of positions not taken are a powerful aid in bringing new or replacement members up to speed, and the residue of factoids known to be false will enable you to efficiently deal later with objections based on things that everybody knows but which did not hold up under investigation. Finally, the study file will capture factoids about which you could not learn anything significant, so you have also documented that which you wished you knew something about but don't.

Use of a study file is especially important when a multidisciplinary team is at work, and holds true through the final narrative. Every discipline has its own jargon, style, and phrases to avoid, and a practitioner can usually tell when something has been written by someone outside their field. When someone detects a clunker in an area they know about, it is likely that they will then distrust all your results.

Using a Wiki makes it easy to capture specialized knowledge in the specialists' own words. Team members can contribute in little dribs and drabs instead of being given a big writing assignment which (in the case of volunteer groups) may be difficult for the most well-intentioned volunteer to find time to do.

Sometimes people try to avoid the overhead of a study file by having the team sit around and converse while some scribe or another take notes, which are then written up afterwards. I've never seen this method produce decent results. No scribe, no matter how skilled at language, can sound as convincing as a true expert; apt metaphors, telling examples, and logical unfolding of narrative only come from people who know what they are writing about.

Gadgets

Team members are going to have to communicate with each other, the study file, and you. They also may have to access the Internet to do searches and solicit information via email, Twitter, and the like.

A common case is a geographically dispersed team of volunteers connected by the public Internet. Each member will come with their own personal way of accessing the Net: laptops and desktops, Macs and PCs and Linux boxes, and now also every flavor of tablet and handheld. Different word processors, different email software, different Web browsers; Flash and no Flash, Java versions all over the place, it goes on and on. Multiply all the options together and you get a major compatibility problem. Documents written by one member have their formats garbled by another member's system. You can't find security software that everybody can use. Backups happen, or don't, depending on the whim of the member. Handhelds favor short emails, messages, and tweets and discourage reading longer, and possibly important blocks of text. Malware can come in from unknown vulnerabilities and go unknown places. The complications never seem to end.

If you have no security problem, then these incompatibilities are at best an annoyance and at worst something that might split the team into factions. If you do have a security problem, they could be fatal.

Looking hard at your communications requirements may show you a few things. One is that the bulk of network use by the team is going to be either the exchange of unformatted text with the study file and each other, or doing Web searches. Another is that a perfectly adequate network gadget equipped with a wireless card can be bought for less than the price of a typical one-way ticket to a team meeting, and a wireless link maintained each month for less than the cost of a team lunch. A dedicated server to host the study file costs far less than the travel expenses of a single team member to a two-day meeting.[50] When you're picking your network gadget you should keep in mind that it will be used as much for content generation as content display, and therefore should have a decent keyboard. It should also be able, if necessary, to support security software such as file encryption.

A dedicated project network, running on dedicated hardware, offers a lot of advantages. You can make sure everything works together, and that anything written by one team member can be read by all without annoying format hassles like those that arise when people use different versions or clones of popular word processors. Emails, draft documents, and search results are isolated from personal data, reducing the chances of inadvertent loss or cross-contamination. You can run backups of both the team members' machines and the server at intervals that are appropriate for the state of the effort at any given time. Having all the elements of the network under your control also makes it feasible to use technical security measures such as encryption.

There is also a psychological advantage to working this way. When team members open their network gadget they get a subconscious message that "now I'm doing study work," and are likely to become more focused as a result.

All the above advice pertains to studies where the team meets in person periodically and communicates electronically between meetings. If the team must operate completely as a "virtual team," with all interactions over a network, then additional hardware and software is required.

Virtual Teams

There's a fair amount of experience out there with virtual software development teams, including multinational ones, and it teaches that it takes more to run a virtual team than just a Wiki and emails.[51]

The basic problem is that teams interact at multiple levels. One level is that of explicit communication about team business. Another level consists of implicit communication through tone of voice, pacing, gesture and facial expression. Yet another has to do with what the team members know about each other and how that influences their interpretation of that second level of communication: when an individual known to be calm under pressure calls in an agitated tone of voice, people know that the matter is important.

Emails and the Wiki work fairly well for the top level, explicit communications but are much, much less effective for the others. If your team is going to be a virtual one, you try very hard to get the members together at periodic, if wide-spaced intervals, and at a minimum hold a kickoff meeting so everybody can see what everybody else looks like. Humans are, after all, social animals.

Once things get going, there will be a need for real-time group discussions, especially when the study reaches the stage where recommendations are being considered. This requires a many-to-many communications facility, as opposed to the one-to-many pattern imposed by email. Options here are conference calls, most economically using Voice Over IP,[52] web conferencing,[53] or, less satisfactorily, collaborative text chat. The latter is supported by a plethora of products,[54] many of which are part of suites that include project management and version control tools. It is important that the discussion support facility be highly reliable and available to all members of the team, or it will act to separate rather than bond individuals. It is unlikely in the extreme that an adequate level of reliability (and security, if needed) will be achieved using a random assortment of team members' personal devices, so for virtual teams it is even more important that identical hardware and software be provided to each member.

Troubling
Thoughts

The thoughts of others
Were light and fleeting,
Of lovers' meeting
Or luck or fame.
Mine were of trouble,
And mine were steady,
So I was ready
When trouble came
—A. E. Housman[55]

If you're lucky, you'll never have to deal with the things discussed in this chapter. If you're prudent, however, you might want to think about the kinds of trouble that might head your way. Just don't overdo it: the ideal state of mind is what we used to call "enlightened paranoia," where enlightenment is the dish and paranoia is the seasoning.

Your first responsibility is to protect the integrity of your process, which means guarding against the loss or corruption of things like the study file. Loss prevention and recovery from accidents is a pretty straightforward business of backups, redundant facilities, and so forth.[56] It is the sort of thing that any reasonably competent system administrator should have at the tips of their fingers.

Secrets

Depending on the nature and subject of your study, you may have a greater or lesser need to keep some information in confidence, if only temporarily. For example, you may be generating proposals or business or product plans, or be given access to other institutions' intellectual property as inputs to your study. You may be required to maintain the privacy of individuals' personal data, such as medical records. Premature release of your recommendations may hurt their chances of being accepted. Total transparency may sound good, but often loses attractiveness when one considers carefully the consequences of certain information being exposed. Even the National Academies, which conducts their studies in a highly transparent fashion, recognizes the need for closed sessions and restricted distribution of intermediate results.[57] Total secrecy, on the other hand, has great potential for concealing mischief, and careful ethical tradeoffs must be considered, as Sissela Bok has done in her excellent study.[58]

Because the word "secret" comes from the same Indo-European root as "discriminate," that which is separated or set apart,[59] it's not surprising that your first step will be to decide what information has to be set aside and subject to restrictions on access.[60] These restrictions should not have the appearance (or reality) of illegal discrimination. You will also need to know the degree to which the backgrounds of your team members can be checked, the degree to which their use of the project network can be monitored, and what limits, if any, are to be imposed on the use of social networks like Facebook, either as part of a background investigation or by members of the team when the study is in progress. Non-compete agreements may be required to protect the interests of the sponsoring organization. There may be non-disclosure agreements to be drafted and determinations made of what constitutes legally adequate trade secret protection.

All this requires dances with lawyers, and like all such entertainments it is wise to know the steps before the music starts.

That Uneasy Feeling

Once you have decided what information needs to be protected from loss or disclosure, then you need to consider the possibility that there exists a threat: some outside agent that is out to get you, either by stealing your material or sabotaging your study.

Threat analysis is about as slippery a topic as you can find. You are never sure that a threat exists until it is too late; you may suspect burglars are operating in your area, but you only really know when you come home and find things missing. As you consider the (usually inadequate) evidence for a threat, you should constantly be asking the question: "What if I'm wrong?"[61] If you say there's a threat, and you're wrong, then you will have paid a "security tax" for nothing. If you say there's no threat, and you're wrong, then either something awful will happen, or an even higher tax will be paid by having one security measure after another hastily imposed as the threat becomes manifest.

Figuring out if somebody would want to steal your stuff is usually fairly straightforward. Figuring out if somebody wants to sabotage your effort may take a little more work. Sabotage is generally motivated either because your study threatens some interest, or for ideological reasons. The Internet is a good place to find indicators of both, especially in the comments sections of specialist and news forums. If your legal dance partner approves, a little careful "trolling," or deliberate insertion of provocative comments, may be used to see if someone could be goaded into attacking a "honeypot," a system of no real value that you set up for just that purpose.[62]

If you do set up a honeypot or engage in other monitoring of potential intrusions, maintain that sense of balance captured in the old military saying "once is chance, twice is coincidence, three times is enemy action."

Countermeasures

If you do decide that someone's out to get you, then you need to estimate how good they are in order to select what you're going to use to keep them out. In the past, one dealt with a range of abilities, with amateurs at the bottom and nation-states at the top; when the bugged typewriters were discovered in 1982 in the American embassy in Moscow, both the location of the typewriters and the electromechanical sophistication of the bugs made it clear that this was a Soviet operation.[63] If you were a commercial firm of no interest to the Soviets, you could pretty much ignore a threat of such sophistication.

This is no longer the case for attacks mounted across the Internet. An active black market in highly advanced malware exists,[64] which means that anybody with intent and a budget can become just about as dangerous as the pros.

That's the bad news.

The good news is that your study has a finite life; even if all your work is to remain secret, after your work is completed your information becomes, in effect, a static archive that can be protected by measures that would be intolerable while the study was under way. Even better news is that the vast bulk of off-the-shelf malware is aimed at popular software. Using systems that are a bit out of the ordinary and adding an overlay of technical countermeasures makes life more difficult for a would-be attacker. That buys you time, and if you buy enough time your study will be over and its remaining valuable information locked away before any potential attacker can get at it.

If your team is in one physical location, then a dedicated workroom with an isolated server and terminals presents a pretty hard target. If your team is dispersed, then you can secure the dedicated network described above by installing encryption software on the team members' gadgets, with a Virtual Private Network[65] to connect them to a physically protected and dedicated server. Don't let any vendor kid you — crypto can be a world class pain. If you don't control every box with crypto on it, there's a good chance it will either slow the team down terribly or, more commonly, cause members to bypass it and turn your security into an illusion. Having all the nodes of the network selected and controlled by you will also enable you to get the bugs out of the system before it's handed to the team, and produce any necessary help files or FAQs.

Finally, remember where the word "secret" comes from. If it looks as if there may be a threat to your study, keep your important information separate: separate from your organization's other data, separate from team members' private data, and above all, separate from the Internet.

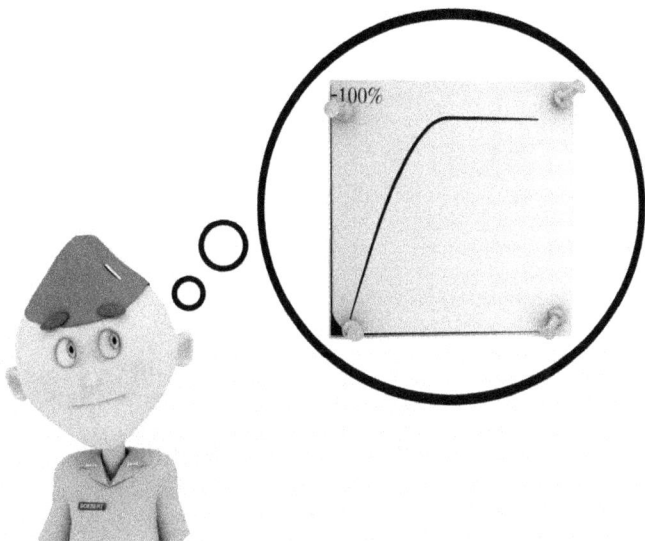

Task
Planning

Plans are worthless, but planning is everything.
—Dwight Eisenhower[66]

As a freshly-minted Air Force Second Lieutenant,[67] I found myself leading a programming project running in parallel with a similar project, that one led by a wily old Master Sergeant. The Colonel[68] insisted that we report progress in terms of percent complete. My curve had the classic look of the newbie: shooting up optimistically at the beginning and then flattening out as things got tough, finally asymptotically approaching 100 percent. The Sergeant managed his curve like it was his stake in a poker game. At each progress report he'd give the Colonel a little percent complete, and if the Colonel complained, he'd give him a little more percent complete the next time. Some people still think percent complete has significance; it was worthless then, and it is worthless today.

Equally useless are the so-called "Gantt Charts" that a lot of automated project management tools crank out in great profusion. These have one axis, time, and line for each task. Little triangles mark when tasks start and end and whether they are slipping. It's important to note that Gantt Charts, and the Critical Path Method they come from, were devised to run military crash projects where schedule was everything and money meant nothing. Your studies probably aren't going to be like that. As a team leader you really need to track your movement through an abstract three-dimensional space, where one dimension is money, one dimension is time, and the third is accomplishment. The best method I know of to do this is called Earned Value Management,[69] and it's worked for me over many years.

Earned Value Management

Those of you who are familiar with the notion of Agile software development[70] are probably thinking "uh-oh, here we go again, 1970s mindset, waterfall diagram, milestones, process over people, yada yada yada." Well, not exactly. If you have all the time and money in the world you don't need to keep track of where you are. If your resources are limited you can be as agile as an acrobat, but if somebody turns out the lights in the middle of your act you haven't done yourself or anybody else any good. So you need to keep track of where you are in that three-dimensional space of time, money, and accomplishment.

Earned Value Management is based on the principle that accomplishment happens in discrete steps, which it calls "milestones." This principle captures the wisdom of Yogi Berra, that "it ain't over 'til it's over."[71] If your task is to drill a hundred holes in a piece of metal, you're not 99 percent done at the 99th hole, because the drill could break off in the piece at the 100th hole.

When you achieve a milestone, then and only then do you check where you are with regard to planned schedule and cost. Since you don't know anything for sure between milestones, (the drill could break in the next hole) you need to set up as many of them as you can.

You find milestones by locating transitions between substantively different activities. They are easy to define and measure when you're building a garage: slab poured, framing up, siding on, etc. It's more difficult, but still possible, when your "thought-stuff" is software: at the very least you can use tests to determine that, say, modules are ready for integration. Defining milestones is very slippery for studies, because measuring accomplishment is all wrapped up in measuring quality. It helps to have external reviewers who can perform a sanity check on the team's assessment of an intermediate product such as a list of findings and recommendations. Given the highly intangible nature of accomplishment in something like a study, don't be surprised if you find yourself using what Herbert Simon called "satisficing,"[72] which in this case means crediting yourself with making a milestone when the results are "good enough" rather than "perfect."

Having a project file is fundamental to deciding whether you've made a milestone or not, because it gives you a body of material to review. If your project information is scattered around in the team members' heads and on their personal machines you won't have a clue as to where you are.

Your milestones will generally coincide with meetings at which the team will evaluate and agree upon the status of results to date. The typical pattern for meetings is that they need to be more frequent at the very beginning, when the team is getting to know each other and brainstorming factoids and issues, and late, when the discussion of recommendations will be intense.

There should be many more reviews of material than those that appear in your task plan; the rule in dealing with "thought-stuff" is small steps, frequent reviews. The plan is there to show you how you're doing with regard to time and money, not to tell you how good your work is, and it probably will be limited by your financial reporting system.

Finally, don't forget to involve the team in task planning and any subsequent replanning, so that everyone shares an understanding of the current project structure and appreciates the reasons tasks and milestones may have to change. People are much more likely to accept changes in their work schedules if they are the ones who suggested them, as opposed to having them dictated from "on high."

The Only Constant is Change

The way to deal with an environment of uncertainty is to update your plan at each milestone. You pretend things are stable and lay out milestones that are intended to carry you to the end, knowing full well that it'll never work out that way. This is the essence of what Eisenhower said: when you plan in detail, you study your situation in enough depth so that when the inevitable emergency arises you can forget your plan and make informed adjustments:

> ... when you are planning for an emergency you must start with this one thing: the very definition of 'emergency' is that it is unexpected, therefore it is not going to happen the way you are planning.

> So, the first thing you do is to take all the plans off the top shelf and throw them out the window and start once more. But if you haven't been planning you can't start to work, intelligently at least. [73]

It's like a movie on film. Each frame is static, but the sequence is dynamic, or, if you prefer, "agile."

A Sample Plan

As an illustration, let's say you have a budget of $100K and schedule of 10 months, and you're doing your first tentative plan.

You plot this on a piece of graph paper that has time on one axis and dollars on the other. So, to continue the example, let's say you give yourself one month for preparatory work, three months to generate and settle issues, two more months to write the first draft, three more months to write the final, and one month to prepare a briefing. That gives you the diagram marked "Step 1." Right away the technique helps because it forces you to explicitly consider how many times you're going to have to iterate specific steps.

Then you decide how much you're going to spend on each task. Let's say $5K to get ready, $25K getting the issues in shape, another $40K to write the first draft, $20K to write the final, and $10K for the briefing. These are represented as targets on the diagram marked "Step 2."

Now you sit and look at that diagram and think very hard about "burn rate:" can you really usefully spend $40K in two months? This will depend

Task Planning: A Sample Plan

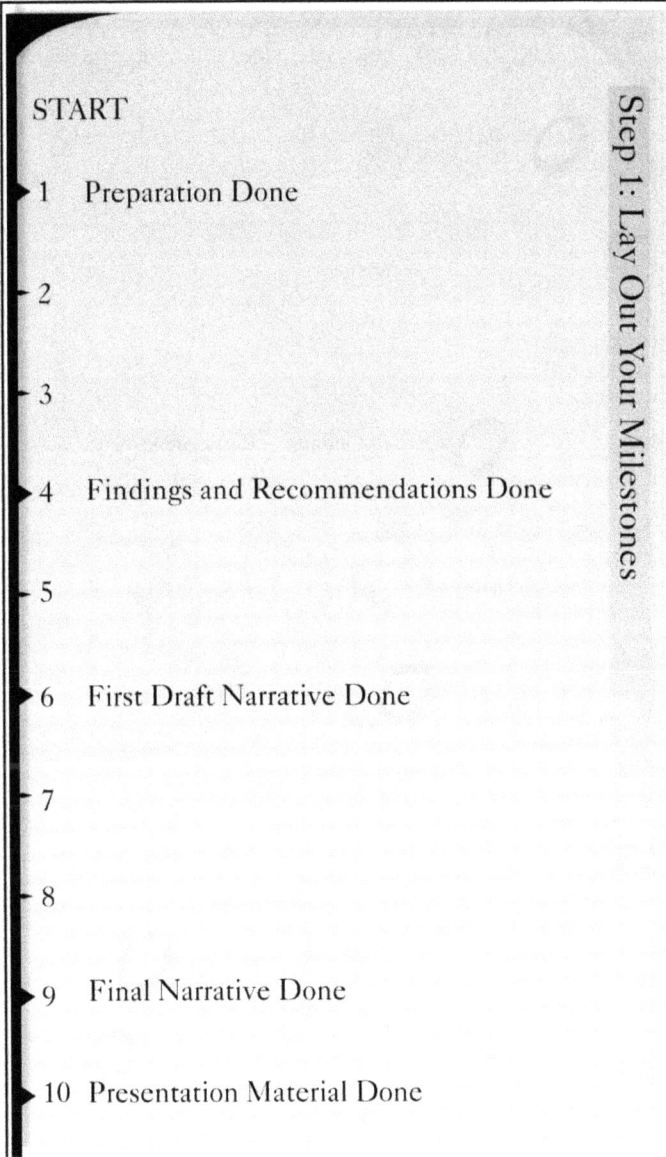

START

1 Preparation Done

2

3

4 Findings and Recommendations Done

5

6 First Draft Narrative Done

7

8

9 Final Narrative Done

10 Presentation Material Done

Step 1: Lay Out Your Milestones

Task Planning: A Sample Plan

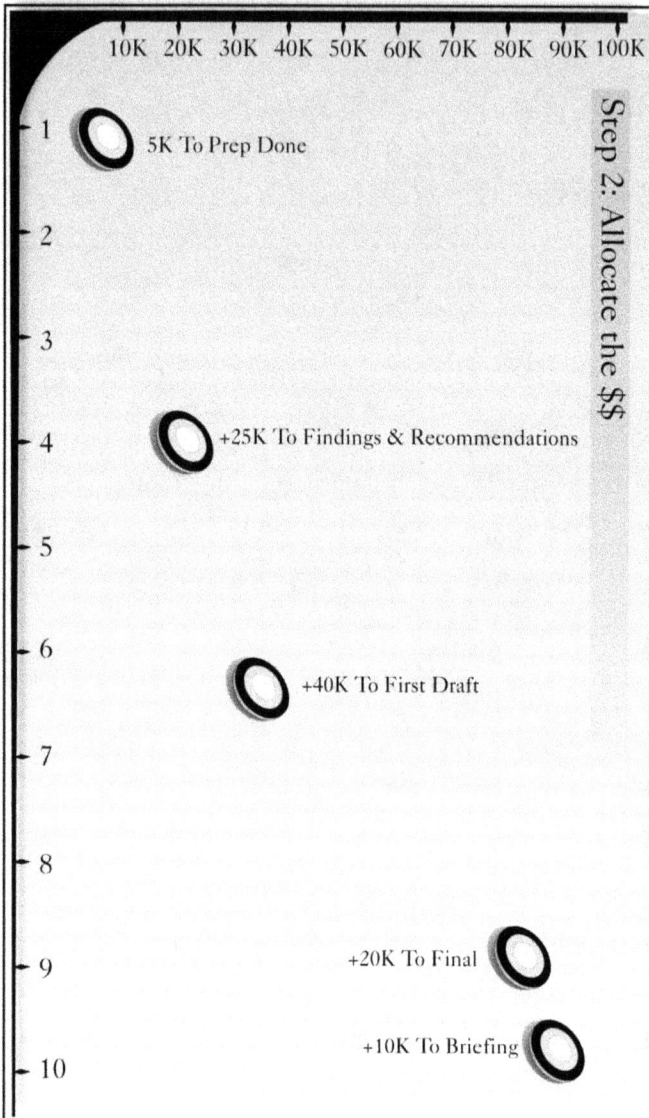

	10K	20K	30K	40K	50K	60K	70K	80K	90K	100K

1 ◯ 5K To Prep Done

2

3

4 ◯ +25K To Findings & Recommendations

5

6 ◯ +40K To First Draft

7

8

9 ◯ +20K To Final

+10K To Briefing ◯

10

Step 2: Allocate the $$

completely on the environment in which you are conducting the endeavor, its priority amongst other projects competing for personnel, whether team members are on board or have to be recruited, and so forth. It's a good idea to do the burn rate by name, that is, to specifically forecast how much of each member's time you are going to require each month.

Once your plan is accepted by you, the team, and other relevant parties, the targets on the chart are used to measure performance against plan. Each target has two values associated with it: one for planned cost, and one for planned date of completion.

Once you have "checked off" a milestone along the accomplishment axis, the formula for determining where you stand with regard to time and money is simple: if you budgeted $5K to reach a milestone, you credit yourself with an Earned Value of $5K when you meet that milestone. If you budgeted $25K to get to the next one, you add $25K when you get there, and so forth.

As each milestone comes up, you compare Earned Value against what you're spending. In these diagrams the light arrows hit where you should be (on target) and the dark ones are where you are. The dotted lines show the nature of your misses: one direction for time

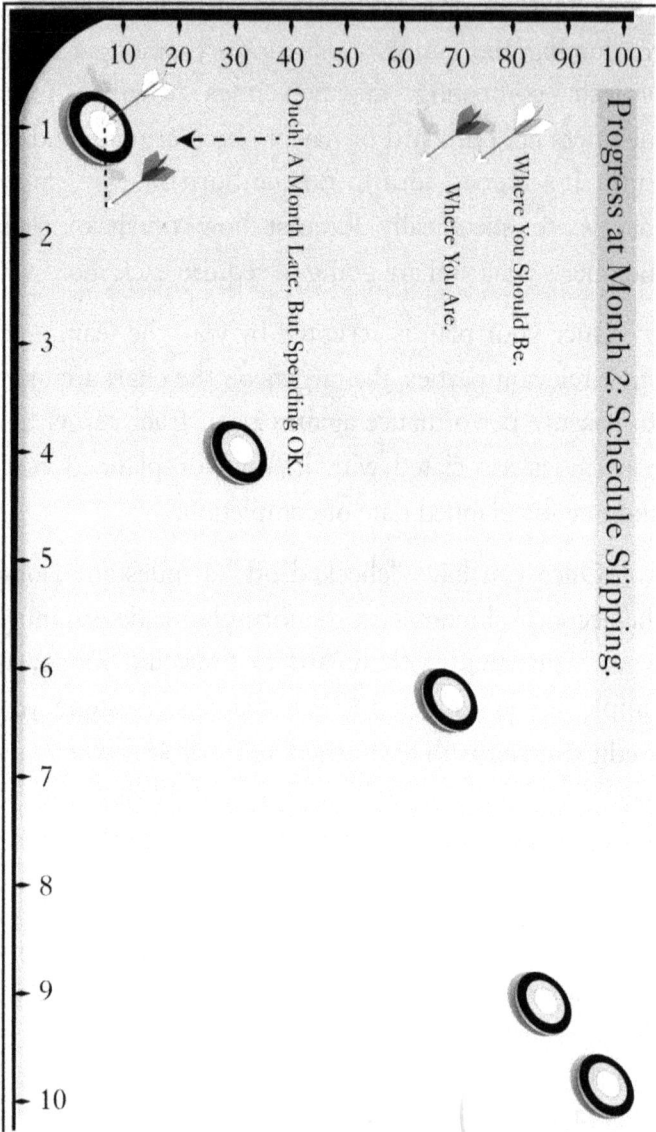

10 20 30 40 50 60 70 80 90 100

Progress at Month 2: Schedule Slipping.

Where You Should Be.

Where You Are.

Ouch! A Month Late, But Spending OK.

and the other for money.

The diagram marked "Progress at Month 2" shows a typical case where you're having trouble getting people on board but your estimate of how much money it would take to get to the first milestone was correct. The result is that you spent the money in two months instead of one. When you credit yourself at the time you make the milestone, your arrow hits at $5K level, which is where your target is, but it's at the two month instead of one month level on the time axis.

Then you add extra people to catch up and spend $30K on the issues, and it still takes three months. When you credit yourself with the $25K value, you get the diagram marked "Progress at Month 5", which shows you that you're both behind schedule and overspent. And so you replan, and try not to miss by so much next iteration.

When you replan you have to decide whether to give the same amount of attention to a smaller problem, or give less attention to the original one. I learned at Honeywell that if you have to cut back it is much better to kill off some task or organization in its entirety than it is to cut a little bit from all of them. Squeezing every activity hurts morale everywhere and

Task Planning: A Sample Plan

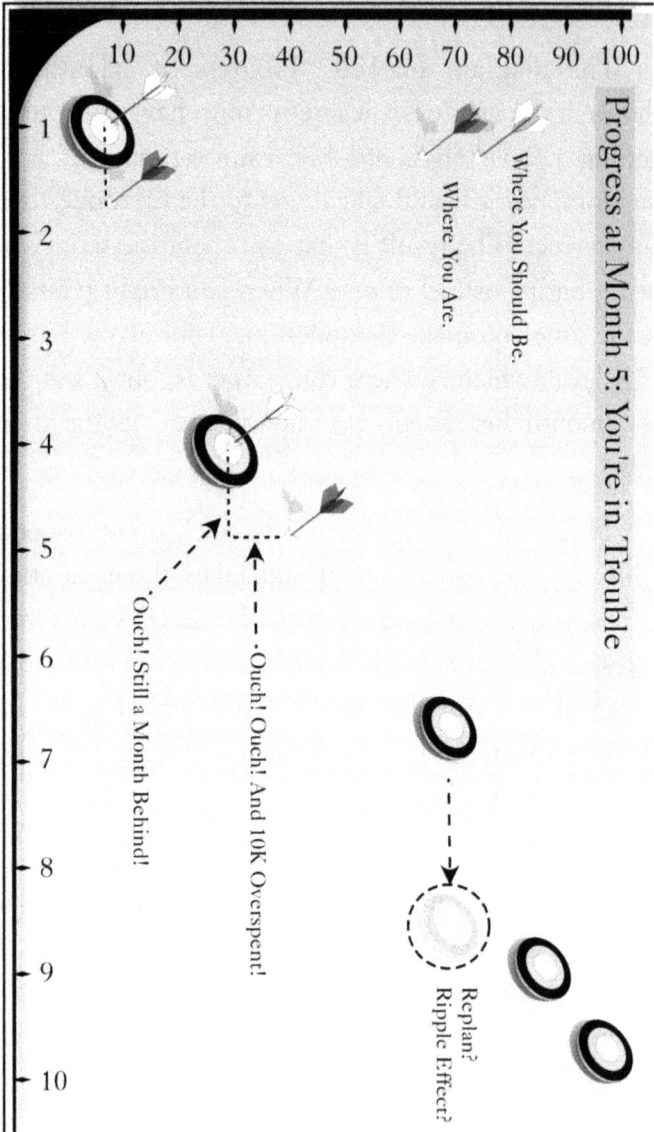

Progress at Month 5: You're in Trouble

10 20 30 40 50 60 70 80 90 100

1

Where You Are.

Where You Should Be.

2

3

4

5

Ouch! Still a Month Behind!

Ouch! Ouch! And 10K Overspent!

6

7

8

9

Replan?
Ripple Effect?

10

causes people to question the viability of the whole effort. So if you look at the last chart, the combination of slippage and overspending has squeezed the task to produce the final version of the narrative. Unless you're really lucky (which you usually aren't) keeping to the same scope of effort will cause this task to slip as well, and the effect will ripple through to the end of the effort. So you either cover fewer topics in a narrative that gets a second version done, or you drop the revision task and ship the first draft.

Like any system, Earned Value Management can be gamed, most commonly by claiming a milestone has been met when the work is not really complete, or by shaving quality. Since you're doing this for your own understanding of how the effort is going, the only person you hurt by cheating is yourself.

And don't get fixated on the mechanics of progress reporting at the expense of progress. As they say in the medical profession, the chart is not the patient.

Now that you have some idea of what you're going to do and who you're going to do it with, it's time to stop thinking about it and start getting on with it.

Work
Your
Plan

Early Days

Meetings, whether physical or virtual, are where you exercise leadership by example. Crisp, disciplined meetings produce crisp, disciplined teams which in turn produce crisp, disciplined results. It's that simple. Get together, exchange information, decide, head for happy hour. You're there to maintain time discipline, log action items for team members, and to be like a frog.

The early meetings of your team are crucial. This is where the team will or will not achieve cohesion, and where the enthusiasm and creativity of the members will be at a peak; people will come in eager to contribute and demonstrate their expertise. The grind comes later, by which time if you've done your job the energy will come from a sense of shared responsibility.

Get a good night's sleep before the kickoff meeting, because you're going to be busy. You will have to explain, and gain support for, the process and schedule. If you took my advice about standard network gadgets you'll need to hand out everybody's new toys and deal with all the sysadmin nits and grits of showing people how the software works, getting users registered and so forth.

The state that takes me the most energy to achieve is being like a frog. The kickoff, and the social event that should be associated with it, is where that lower, implicit level of communication between team members begins as they begin to know each other and recognize their similarities and differences. You need to be alert to what the interactions between members tell you about their personalities, and help the relationships begin. There will be times during some of these events that you will feel more like a cruise ship social director than a team leader, but trust me, it's all in aid of progress.

You'll work hardest at this when there is a wide disparity in age, seniority, and experience between team members. Senior members may expect deference, and tend to dominate conversations, but often the junior members are far closer to the realities of the topic under study.

Once the team has settled in and gotten used to each other and the tools, it's time to start the brainstorming, or, as one of my co-workers called it, Le Grand Spew. The idea here is for people to just throw out potential factoids and issues as fast as they can, no matter how strange and off the wall they may seem. You want to get the interactions between the team members to cause mental sparks to fly. Brainstorming always works best when everybody is in the same room. If you are leading a virtual team, this is the time to blow your travel budget.

No evaluation of ideas is permitted, and no stopping to sharpen the wording; that will come later. During this exercise you just jot down the gist of the idea as best you can along with the name of its source. At the end of the meeting you go down through these, asking each person to post their ideas to the study file.

While brainstorming, members may propose what they think are issues but what are really positions, e.g., "let's use Linux," when the issue is really "What operating system should we use?" It's important not to point this out at the time the proposal first appears, as this will divert the group away from the rapid generation of ideas. Just make sure it gets captured in the study file and sort it out after the collective creative burst has died down.

It's likely that your team will conform to the 80/20 rule: 80 percent of the work will be done by 20 percent of the team. You get to work overtime to make sure those people are not overloaded with trivial tasks.

After a couple of meetings you'll start to appreciate the value of that study file as a way of keeping the team on track. I think we've all been on teams where one member brings up the same tired issue over and over again. This may be because you've got a rabid hedgehog on your hands. On the other hand, it may be a symptom that your meeting is out of control, and the person fears an important issue is going to be overlooked. You can often get things back on track with a gentle reminder such as "we've got that captured as Issue Fourteen; is the current wording correct?" If the answer is "no," then you suggest that the individual fix it — turning complaints into action items is a good way to see just who's in the productive 20 percent. If the answer is "yes" then the team can move on. In any case this is better for team cohesion than some variation of "shut up, we've heard it before," no matter how felicitously stated. Unstructured meetings favor the glib and superficial, whereas what you should be looking for are the deep and profound.

As things progress, your meetings will roughly follow Robert's Rules of Order: old business (reviewing existing factoid and issue wording) followed by new business (things people have thought up since last time). Team members should be prepared by having read the factoid and issues files in advance. If you have deadwood who refuse to do their homework, my advice is to get rid of them if you can, and find something else for them to do if you can't, because slacking off is a contagious disease.

Factoids
Into
Findings

*The beginning of wisdom is finding out
what you don't know.*
—*Sam Adams*[75]

Turning factoids into findings is one of the most enjoyable parts of a study. It's an evolutionary process that practically runs itself, driven by the team members' curiosity and love of solving puzzles. Disputes are rare, and can generally be settled by digging deeper or, at worst, agreeing to disagree.

The evolution is a more complex process than "connecting the dots." It is more like the uncovering of a mosaic, like something reconstructed from a Roman villa. The process consists first of collecting all the pieces, then painstakingly assembling them into a picture. One proceeds first by matching individual pieces by simple criteria such as color, then gradually a fragment of, say, an eyebrow appears, which both gives a partial result (this is a portrait) and sharpens your search criteria (we're looking for pieces of a face).

Now it is possible that E.D. Morel had the true nature of the Congo Free State revealed to him something like the scene in bad adventure movies when they open the box and the blue light pours out, but I doubt it; his writing just shows too much intellectual power.[76] Using the labels I have introduced earlier, I think it went something like this:

Morel began by accepting Leopold and his henchmen's appeal to Categorizing Mind, and assigned the label "humanitarian" to the Congo Free State. He then, consciously or otherwise, began putting the mosaic of such an enterprise in his mind, assembling factoids from his experience in the shipping business, his visits to Brussels, and the lists of what was going in and out of Leopold's colony. Looking at this evidence with Beginner's Mind, he saw that something that should have been there wasn't: compensation going in for ivory coming out. And then he realized that Leopold's label was a lie.

Flaky Factoids

Expect to encounter a lot of factoids whose sources are more or less suspect. Rants on blogs and forums, rumors, blatant propaganda, spin, and general weirdness tossed at you in person and over the Internet.

Liars and con artists usually show up when money is involved, such as when you're doing a business plan, looking for a subcontractor for a proposal, or making recommendations for the funding of one thing or another. They can be pretty good at what they do: fooling people. The most dangerous of these are the mythomaniacs; they not only fool others, they fool themselves. You could strap them to a theoretically perfect lie detector and it would show no deception.

When something sounds or looks like it was designed to mislead, just remember how con jobs work: they always begin on a firm foundation of truth — it's the extrapolation that kills you.[77]

The spin doctors are more subtle. These people seldom lie explicitly because it's too easy to get caught. Instead, they are economical with the truth; they omit things, what's known in the legal profession as *suppressio veri,*[78] and what stage magicians call misdirection.

Even lies and attempts to lead you to a predefined conclusion can convey useful information, if contemplated with Beginner's Mind. For example, let's say a talking dog stops you on the street, jumps up and puts his paws on your chest, and lays an intriguing factoid on you. Now what?

One option is to reject that factoid out of hand, because no sane person listens to talking dogs.

The other is to forget where that factoid came from and chase it down. The frog doesn't care if a fly got there on its own power, was shipped by FedEx, or came down a transporter beam from the Starship Enterprise: if it looks edible and it's within range, it's lunch. It's your Categorizing Mind that wants to put a "flaky" label on that factoid. Instead, go after it with Beginner's Mind. It may be dead wrong, or it may be almost right, containing either a germ of truth that attempting to refute it will uncover, or it will point in a fruitful direction. The latter is often the case with suspected scams and spin, where a valuable question may be: "if they want me to look at this, what is it that they don't want me to look at?"

103

The Tubes of the Interwebs

Like most everything, the Internet ain't what it used to be. When I first went on line in 1972, it was a research network called the ARPAnet, owned by the government and run by universities. There were less than 30 nodes and you had to have a note from your mother (er, government sponsor) to get an account. The ARPAnet was full of facts, there were no search engines as we know them now, and you had to ask around to find stuff. This had the side benefit that you met a lot of fascinating people in your area of interest.

Later, say up to 2005 or so, there was a time when search engines were really useful because the ratio of substance to advertisement was still pretty good. Now you have to wade through a lot of spam and dreck to find the nuggets you want. Worse, people are now spoofing the search engine algorithms to get advertisement- (or malware-) loaded sites to the top of the results. The result is a paradise of false positives and possibly the greatest time-waster ever issued from the hand of man.

Internet answers tend to be quick, but how good are they? Sturgeon's Law[79] says that ninety percent of everything is crap; when it comes to the Internet, I think that's wildly optimistic. Examples abound, but here's one I just ran into in the course of writing this book. I was trying to locate the source of the Thomas Carlyle quote I used as an epigraph for the Foreword. I had run across the quote on the Internet as beginning "by nature, man hates change." Searching on that got three thousand hits and no source. It turns out that's because that version is a misquote; the one I give is right, and, it yields only a couple of hundred hits. There are two morals to this story: link count is not an indicator of truth, and dig until you hit bedrock, then document where that rock came from. Finding good factoids is not a variant of one-click shopping.

There are, however, several tricks that can help your team avoid rattling around in the tubes forever.

One timesaver is to start with the specialist forums where people who know what they are talking about meet and exchange ideas.[80] Because they typically get few links, they usually show up at the bottom of search engine results, so you can save time by starting at the last page and working forward.

Another trick is to process lengthy documents through "tag cloud" software to squeeze the fat out of them. The illustration below is a tag cloud for a GAO report on FAA modernization.[81]

achieve address agency **air** aircraft airports airspace
atc aviation **capacity** challenges
controllers cost **delays** deploy efficient
equipment expected **faa** facilities
flight free help important **increase**
industry initiatives **major**
modernization nas nation
performance plan **problems** program
projects route **system**
technologies traffic

The larger the word, the more frequently it appears in the document. It's a quick way to identify documents that are mostly jargon and MBA-speak. There are multiple places on the Web that generate these.[82]

A common source of false positives is the "meme of the day," some flaky factoid that goes viral through Twitter and Facebook and ends up being one of those things that everybody knows all about — except for the fact that it's wrong. A good example was the incorrect Martin Luther King Jr. quote that splattered all over the Net in response to the killing of Osama Bin Laden.[83] One way to filter these out is to use the "date range" option on Google searches to make sure that the hits you get are within a plausible period and not just things that all popped up yesterday.

Another potential problem results from the recording of browsing histories, which are then used to modify search results to fit the preferences of person using that browser.[84] It is not clear at the time of writing how prevalent such tailoring is, but you should be aware that the possibility, at least, is there. Avoiding being trapped by such "helpful" biases on the part of search engines requires that you distrust the search engine's ordering of the results and go through all of them. The biasing software, of course, does not have a human identity to work from but rather "fingerprints" your browser by leaving information on your system or examining characteristics such as the software or fonts you have installed. If the practice of biasing search results becomes widespread, it will provide another argument for providing a standard network gadget to team members, which will not have the history (and corresponding biases) associated with their personal machines.

And, finally, there's every lazy student's friend: Wikipedia. It should be used with care. It's seldom wrong, but often incomplete, and for your purposes has the worse shortfall that it doesn't tell what factoids have been rejected and why. The first place you should turn to in a Wikipedia article is the history file. This will give you an idea of how much "churn" there is in the article and how controversial the subject is. You get the latter from seeing how much "vandalism" has been backed out by the editors. In any case, don't treat Wikipedia as an authority, but just as one more talking dog on the Internet.

The Future is Hard to See

Every recommendation carries with it an implied prediction: do this and things will be better. Sometimes the prediction is explicit and quantified, as when public policy or finance is involved: mortality rates will decrease by so much, we'll all get rich by this much, and so forth.

There is a growing trend to use mathematical or computer models to perform these extrapolations from one kind of data set or another. These models are seductive, especially when they produce pretty pictures or animations. They have great appeal to people without a background in mathematics or statistics, who tend to take mathematics more seriously than mathematicians do, and assume that it is a source of absolute truth. Just remember that predictive models have the basic structure of a con job, starting with verifiable fact and then extrapolating out into the unknown. The difference is in intent; the con artist wants to fool you, whereas the model builders may be fooling themselves.

The subtlety of modeling was best expressed by Alan Turing, in one of the last papers he wrote before his death:

> *... a mathematical model of the growing embryo will be described. This model will be a simplification and an idealisation, and consequently a falsification. It is to be hoped that the features retained for discussion are those of greatest importance in the present state of knowledge.* [85]

Or, as one eminent statistician admitted: "All models are wrong, but some are useful."[86]

It can be very difficult to figure out what has been falsified by omission, or, if you want to sound like a Ph.D., "abstracted out." Another problem arises from models which require probabilities as input, such as the probability of failure or the probability of an attack happening. Such models are useful for "what if" analysis where you see what happens if you vary the input probabilities. Trying to get a hard answer out of such models often degenerates into educated guesswork.

People have built mathematical models of financial markets that abstract out emotion[87] despite long-standing evidence that such markets are primarily driven by greed and fear.[88]

Worse, models may implicitly or explicitly assume a continuous universe and ignore the possibility of the unusual, catastrophic events that have come to be called "Black Swans."[89]

Given that even the people who devise these things may not know their limitations — note that Turing carefully said he "hoped" he had retained what was important — how should you use mathematical models in your search for valid findings? I suggest that unless your grasp of statistical theory is firm enough to allow you to cross swords with the Bayesians,[90] don't waste time trying to figure out if a model has omitted anything important. Instead, view the model as yet another talking dog: "interesting tip, we'll look into it."

Getting
To
Recommendations

It is a capital mistake to theorise before one has data.
Insensibly one begins to twist facts to suit theories,
instead of theories to suit facts.
—A. Conan Doyle[1]

In contrast to findings, which evolve, recommendations are consciously constructed at one time by the exercise of judgement supported by the findings.

The tool for doing this is the decision tree, which is a kind of flow chart that lays out the sequence of how you're going to decide. So the process of getting to recommendations involves two steps: first construct the decision tree, and then "walk" it to the selected end points, each of which will be a recommendation.

Going about things this way helps keep you from overlooking things, forces convergence on a set of issues, and most importantly, gives the team specific decisions to be made one at a time and in sequence, which inhibits the all-too-common failure mode of going back over old issues until the time and money runs out.

Decision trees can be formal and quantitative,[92] or informal and qualitative. The latter kind is the one I've used most often, just a rough sketch of the issues that must be decided on the path to a given recommendation.

Just as findings require explicit consideration of what isn't there, recommendations require explicit consideration of the paths not to be taken. This often requires that you take into account not just the actual cost of doing something, but the "opportunity cost" of what you decided not to do.

Opportunity Cost

One issue many people seem to overlook (or not want to face) is the question of opportunity cost. It's an old concept, going back to at least the 1840s. Economists have formalized it into something that only other economists can understand, but there is a common sense definition that is applicable to the affairs of ordinary mortals. The basic idea is that managing in a world of finite resources is a zero-sum game. This really hits you when you're managing a startup company. You get an initial investment from the venture capitalists and that's it until you hit your initial financial objectives. For every thing that you decide to do, there's some other potentially valuable thing you can't do because you've spent the money someplace else. You can just let that happen, or (more wisely) you can incorporate opportunity cost into your decision making.

Either/Or, or In Between

Opportunity cost comes in two flavors: either/or decisions, which are often simple, and tradeoffs, which often aren't.

For example, if the problem is one of crossing a river, a top level issue is whether to use a bridge or a ferryboat; if the team selects bridge, then there are a lot of issues about boat design and implementation that are no longer relevant — although consideration of them, and the difficulties and risk they involve, may have influenced the decision to go with a bridge.

On the other hand, it may not be a case of picking one and rejecting the other. Let's say you're the Chief Security Officer for a junkyard. You have a fixed budget which isn't going to go up — it's a tough business, and the boss views security as a cost item that puts no money in his pocket. Your options are to spend your money on dogs or a fence. If you get more dogs, then you don't get as high a fence. If you build up the fence, you can afford fewer dogs. So you have to juggle both until you reach some kind of a balance.

A diagram showing a tradeoff space captures the essence nicely. In our example, that would be a two

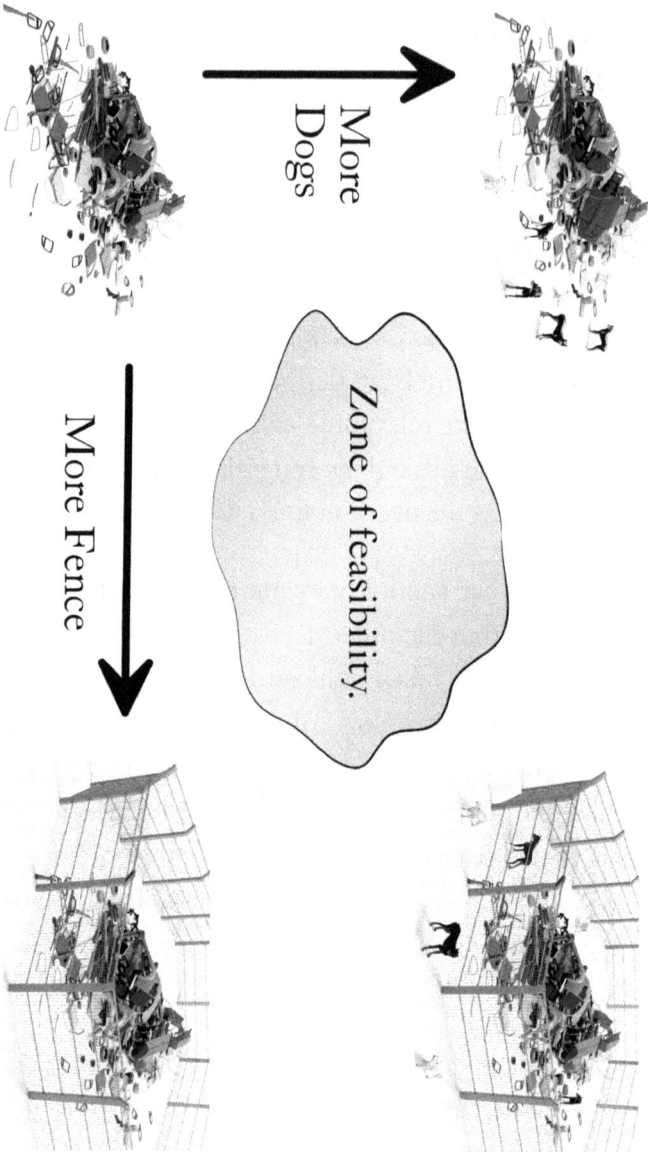

More Dogs

More Fence

Zone of feasibility.

dimensional space with number of dogs on one axis and options for fence design arranged in order of increasing cost on the other. Within that space there will be a "zone of feasibility." The lower left corner is no dogs, no fence and no security: clearly unacceptable. The opposite corner is maximum dogs and maximum fence: clearly unaffordable. The corner with all dogs and no fence means there is nothing to slow down an intruder and give the dogs a chance to get there. The corner with all fence and no dogs means that once the intruder gets over the fence they are free to do what they wish. So the answer is somewhere in the middle. Within this zone there will be a set of practical dog-to-fence spending ratios on which to base a rational recommendation.

Prefacing the list of options with a discussion of the tradeoff space will demonstrate that the team has thought hard about the structure of the problem, which, of course, is what preparing the chart will have forced it to do.

It may be the case that you don't have the resources to actually conduct the tradeoff analysis; often it is the case that essential quantitative data has to be dug up.

Pruning the Tree

You should find that the tradeoff issues will end up at the end of a branch, and not in the middle of a cluster. In the junkyard example, you might have an either/or issue of whether to have your own security force or outsource the yard's security to a different company. A dog/fence tradeoff diagram would obviously only be relevant if you decided to do your own security. Then the tradeoff space "hangs off" the end of the branch of having your own force.

You may also not have the time nor the money within the scope of your study to actually do the tradeoff analysis, but rather you recommend the option that requires it (in house security) and outline how it should be done (dogs vs. fence). You also need to describe the issues involved in the analysis: what data is required, and how one would tell whether a particular point is or is not in the zone of feasibility.

As far as the mechanics of the process goes, I used to build decision trees on a table (or, for large ones, on the floor of the "boiler room") using 3 x 5 cards, one issue per card, with the supporting factoid forming a little deck underneath each issue.[93] This makes it easy to shuffle the issues around until you're satisfied with the tree.

And don't get mechanical about all this. These steps are intended to clarify your thinking, not act as a substitute for it.

Embrace Dissent

As a team leader, it is important to have some formal mechanism whereby team members can have dissenting views incorporated into the narrative. The actual form of the dissent can be as a footnote, an appendix, or a separate minority report. The fact that the team members know dissent will be accommodated has, in my experience, the effect of reducing chances of it actually happening.

The big danger in any consensus-based decision process is falling into "groupthink,"[94] where a team bonds too tightly and becomes a kind of collective Categorizing Mind, unable to break out of a language trap of their own devising. Dissent is an antidote to that, and you should insure that the dissenters are heard, no matter how unpleasant the message or personally obnoxious the dissenter; it is wise to remember that pearls begin as an irritant.

As a team member, you may come to the uncomfortable conclusion that your study is a train wreck, but its subject is too important for you to just quit. In such cases I advise against dissenting about everything that bothers you, because to an outside observer you stand a good chance of coming across as an all-around malcontent. Instead, you should very carefully decide what is your single most important issue, and focus all your effort on getting that single message across. If you dissent, and it later turns out you were right, then the only thing I can say is that cold comfort is better than no comfort at all.

Stay Grounded

I hope you realize that dragons actually existed. The evidence from artists and chroniclers worldwide is overwhelming. Once you accept this, figuring out the details is straightforward.

Studying the depictions of dragons in the literature we observe that given the small size of their wings, both wing and power loadings would be too great for them to sustain aerodynamic flight; plus it is clear from paintings, drawings, and tapestries that they could hover. The obvious alternative to powered or gliding flight is that they were lighter than air, that is, living dirigibles having a metabolism that filled them with hydrogen gas. Once this insight is gained then the other characteristics of dragons are readily explained. Their fiery breath comes from venting hydrogen to maintain aerostatic balance. Internal pressure and extremely light skeletal structure explain their vulnerability to piercing weapons such as lances and spears. The extreme lightness of their skeletal structures explains why no fossils have been found. They excrete hydrochloric acid, which explains why they lined their nests with gold. All this is exquisitely documented in a classic of its field.[95]

In a similar spirit, and in reaction to the systems engineering faddism prevalent in the 1970s, I developed at that time a top-down modular decomposition of an antigravity machine. It was all there: control room, inertial platform, sensor suite, the works. The interfaces to the gravity vector reversal module were defined to a level of detail worthy of a build-to specification. After I presented it in a design class there were people in the Systems Engineering Department who wouldn't speak to me for weeks.

These are examples of traps you can fall into, especially when one of your recommendations is "design and build a new gizmo that looks like this." The trap is built by your Categorizing Mind, which is perfectly happy to stay inside a closed system that is detached from reality. The trap is baited by how easy it is to sell something like an antigravity machine. There are a few things you can do to avoid these traps. A technical proposal (which is, in effect, what you are producing with this kind of recommendation) should contain a section in which the critical technical problem is identified and at least partially worked out; for the antigravity machine, the internals of the gravity vector reversal module would be of the greatest interest to a skeptical observer. If software is involved, and you present a small prototype to demonstrate feasibility, then you should also present evidence that the solution will scale to the desired environment. If you can't produce hard numbers for this, you may be in a more risky situation than you think. It's likely that you will not have the resources to produce a full specification of the gizmo, but at the very least you should produce a concept of operations[96] which presents scenarios to show what your gizmo will and won't do, how it will react to operator inputs (if any) and, most importantly, how it might fail and what the consequences of failure would be.

Love Hurts

Last thing before you launch into the narrative phase: look at your findings and recommendations with Beginner's Mind. Do the findings indicate the situation is dire, but the recommendations are timid? Conversely, do the findings show that incremental improvement is called for, but the recommendations call for radical transformation? Have you honestly covered the impact of opportunity costs, or are your recommendations biased toward potential benefits without adequate emphasis on what isn't to be done? Has anyone ever done what you are recommending before, and if so, how did it turn out? This last question is a good way to detect if your team has been seduced by the latest academic or management fad.

Think Dirty

My father had a first-class criminal mind. He was a railroad policeman and claims agent, and he could tell you every method there was for defrauding, sabotaging, or stealing from a railroad. I don't think he received so much as a traffic ticket his entire life.

Thinking dirty is different from acting dirty:

There is a great deal of difference between a person who chooses not to sin and one who doesn't know how.[97]

Thinking dirty is a way of avoiding unintended side effects of well-meaning recommendations, especially in the area of public policy. Clean thinkers look at a policy proposal and ask "how can this help?" Dirty thinkers look at the same proposal and ask "how can this be abused?" You may view them as cynics or realists, but even a nodding acquaintance with history will convince you of the human capacity for mischief.

You subject your results to dirty thinking by having a group first brainstorm possible ways of exploiting what you have recommended, then you see you can address them with refined recommendations and have the group take another crack at it. It's essentially the same process by which "almost right" factoids are refined. It's different and harsher than just having an outside review group (which is also a good idea) in that the group has an objective: to see if it is possible twist, distort, and pervert your recommendations in ways that run counter to your true intent. Going through this exercise may save you from embarrassment at the least and tragic error at worst.

Pray for Peace, Plan for War

In late 1970, right after Honeywell bought the General Electric computer business, I was dispatched to Boston to check out a joint GE-MIT venture called Multics.[97] My boss at the time strongly hinted that I should write a report saying that Honeywell should kill it. I went out, was deeply impressed, and wrote a report saying that Honeywell should invest in it and consider it as the basis of a new product line.

I was caught flatfooted by the reaction to my memo. I had completely underestimated the degree to which the GE corporate culture resembled Italy under the Borgias. Those of us who saw Multics as the technology of the future found ourselves in the fight of our lives against supporters of the established GE operating system, an obsolescent construct known as GCOS. We were constantly on the defensive, and our defeat was sealed when funding was allocated away from Multics to a new follow-on to GCOS, a project which, as we predicted, came to nothing. All this, of course, took place prior to the advent of the Apple II and the IBM PC, the point which most people think of as the dawn of the computer age. Had we prevailed, your computer might look quite different today. You wouldn't get that silly prompt asking you if you wanted to save your work when closing an application, most common attacks would be unheard-of, and you wouldn't have to stop working while your software was being updated.

This was the point where I entered the career version of the Great Doubt, and I vowed I would never make the same mistake again. After that, every time I found myself proposing some course of action that had the slightest chance of being opposed by some faction or another, I prepared in my own mind a political strategy to overcome that opposition. I never again went in to a potential controversy assuming that all it took to prevail was being right. I advise you to think the same way: if your study is worth doing, it will prompt change, and change can be threatening. Just make sure your political strategy is an adjunct to, and not a replacement for, getting it right.

Getting
The
Word Out

... perfection is finally attained not when there is no longer anything to add, but when there is no longer anything to take away ...
— *Saint-Exupéry*[99]

If you've done the preceding steps you should be in pretty good shape with regards to content. You should know what you know and why you know it, what you don't know but wished you did, what you are going to tell people they should do and and the opportunity costs associated with what you're telling them not to do. Now the job is to mold this content into a compelling narrative. The first task usually is to capture all this in some kind of a document.

Writing It Up

There are two general ways to go about producing a document: outline-first or text-first.

Outline-first means you do the structure first and then fill in the outline with text. Text-first writing is a microcosm of the study process of the endeavor: first you generate small blocks of text, then you assemble them into a coherent whole. Once you know what text you have in hand, then you figure out where the blocks should go, and finally smooth out the transitions.

If you've reached this point by the path I've described, you already have your blocks of text in the study file, and they should have been reviewed and wordsmithed to a fare-thee-well. The remaining work should be the top-level organization and "bridge text" I've described above. If it isn't, then you're in trouble.

All the great disasters of document preparation I have been involved with have come from trying to proceed outline-first; all the best documents I've written were done text-first.

I think the reason for this is twofold: first, when you're fiddling with the outline you're burning time and money without producing text, which means the pace at which you must write to meet your deadlines increases the more you fiddle. This in turn leads to hurried and sloppy writing, and in the worst case means you hit your deadline with nothing to deliver. Second, I firmly believe that the underlying structure of a narrative is discovered, not invented. As you work with the text you start discovering the order of presentation that gets your message across smoothly and forcefully. Great documents present their ideas in an elegant sequence in which each new concept builds on its predecessors — just don't think for a moment that they were written in that sequence.

It's best if you, as team leader, do the first draft. You should be the person with the broadest understanding, and you will also eventually be the person to present and defend this narrative to its intended audience. The first draft will be rough, it will stumble, and everybody will hate it. Don't defend it, fix it. Lapidary prose comes from the lapidary process: polish, polish, and polish some more.

A tedious but essential task is the construction of the "scholarly apparatus," the notes which direct the reader to the sources of your knowledge. This is not just showing off; without references your report will come across as just another infomercial or political screed, no matter how true it may be in fact. If your report is being read by people with scholarly training or instincts, the first thing they are likely to do is turn to the back and examine the references. If your references are scanty, biased, or in the worst case nonexistent, then many individuals whom you most want to reach may read no further.

The Internet has generated new and as yet unresolved difficulties with regard to references. Beside the obvious barbarism of the typical URL format, much useful information on the Web is ephemeral and may disappear before some interested reader can access it. There isn't much that can be done about URLs, but you should maintain an archive of the Web pages you've referenced in case some researcher asks for them in the future.

Be Blunt

At one point in my Air Force tour I sat in a briefing promoting the then-new counterinsurgency doctrine, which was just beginning to become a big deal. The briefing was a slick collection of abstractions: charts and graphs of sorties flown, bombs dropped, insertions made, seasoned with hearts and minds and hamlets. It was the whole McNamara catastrophe in a nutshell: war as an exercise in statistical quality control.[100] Sitting next to me was someone who had won a chest full of medals fighting in Burma in World War II.[101] His face grew darker with every upward pointing chart. Finally he leaned over to me and said in a stage whisper "I fail to see what all this has to do with jumping out of airplanes and sticking knives in people."

That one whisper blew away all the pretense and puffery in the room. It was blunt, it was factual, and it was forceful, the way you should especially be if your study involves life and death. Don't say "less than optimum validation may lead to adverse outcomes," say "if we get this wrong people are going to die." Leave the abstraction and weasel words to the politicians and spin doctors.[102]

Master the Basics

One day Katagiri Roshi gave a demonstration of calligraphy. During it he explained that in the traditional method of teaching Japanese calligraphy, students were required to duplicate exactly the teacher's style before they were permitted to develop their own. That's probably a bit extreme for Western culture, but the approach is a good one: learn by emulating the people whose work you admire, then put your own personality on what you do.

If your writing is so bad that you are inhibited by the fear that people are going to make fun of you, then there are two things you have to learn. At the bottom level you need to know how to construct a proper sentence. There are books and online resources that can help you with that. [103,104] If you're really lost, the absolute best way to learn the structure of an English sentence is to first learn how to diagram them,[105] then find sentences you like and diagram those. Tedious at first, but if you stick to it you will get the hang of it quickly. Churchill, who was no slouch at writing, referred to "words fitting and falling in their places like pennies in a slot."[106] Once you get the knack of sentence construction you can concentrate on your thoughts without constantly worrying if you are going to come across as an illiterate.

The next thing to learn is structure, how you organize the narrative in such a way that the reader absorbs what you are saying smoothly and completely, without stumbling over omissions or loose ends. That's a harder skill to acquire, but the approach to learning is the same: read, analyze, emulate. Then break out on your own.

One good exercise is to go to the *New York Times* or similar archive, pick a topic of interest to you, and find a long article written during the golden age of newspaper writing, say, from 1930 to 1950 or so. Those newspaper people knew how to write to a deadline and get a message across without wasting words.

Summarize the paragraphs, study their sequence, and examine how evidence is put forth. Go up to the next level and distill out the author's objectives. Then paste it into your word processor and see if you can improve it.

If your study is in support of government policy, a good document to study is George Kennan's famous

"Long Cable,"[107] which set the direction of American foreign policy for the duration of the Cold War. It is a classic of exposition, well worth taking apart to see how it was put together.

Capture the Skimmers

Today's world is one of ever decreasing attention span and ever increasing distraction. Because of that, you must pay special attention to getting your message across to people who are fast forwarding through your text. The longer your document and the more complex your argument, the more important it is to capture the skimmers.

The most basic tool for doing this is the Executive Summary. This is the one place where bulletized lists work. Each "bullet point" should be short, one or two sentences, and as punchy as you can make it. Give page numbers or other links to the relevant sections. Your objective should be to provoke the reader into going deeper, even if it's only into part of the report. Always include an Executive Summary; otherwise your report may be summarized by some staffer on the receiving end, which means you just lost control of your message.

Your illustrations can be put to good use here. *Scientific American* magazine used to have an editorial policy that a reader should be able to get the gist of an article from just the captions to the pictures. The modern layout doesn't go quite that far, but they still load a lot of information in and around the pictures — and it still works. A master of print advertising[108] once observed that everyone reads the headline to an ad, and that you shouldn't be shy about putting a lot of information there.

If you are blessed with good illustrations (and you should work to insure this is the case) then a good way to organize your document is to storyboard it like a movie, where your pictures are the scenes. Then put a caption under each, not worrying about length. Once that tells your story then you can interpose the more detailed text. Likewise, your chapter and section headers should present the irreducible core of your argument.

Finally, typography helps catch the eye. Subtle differences in typeface attract the eye; *Scientific American* is worth studying in this regard. As with your prose, don't overdo it. If people are thinking "what a cool use of typography" instead of "that's clearly what we should do," then they're thinking about the package instead of its contents.

Show Business

The Air Force of my day ran on kerosene, alcohol, and numbers. The kerosene went into the airplanes, the alcohol went into the officers, and the numbers went to General Curtis E. LeMay,[109] who ran the outfit. He was a bear for quantified measures of effectiveness, and God help you if you fell short: he'd sack you in less than a heartbeat. Everyone who served under him knew his motto that "I do not have the time to distinguish between the unfortunate and the incompetent."[110] One mistake and you would be posted to some distinctly unpleasant location, and in the 1960s the USAF had plenty to choose from. It was not a serene environment.

LeMay was a techie at heart, and he loved the idea of computers, or Electronic Data Processing as it was called then, and in the early 1960s he pushed automation at a rate commensurate with a "peacetime Air Force on a wartime footing."[111] Programming experience was rare in 1962 and even rarer in the Air Force. First assignments after commissioning were made by Air Training Command, who sent me to (surprise!) Headquarters Air Training Command. At that time, ATC was just a bit smaller than all of IBM Corporation worldwide.[112] As a Lieutenant I occupied a position that the organization chart said should be occupied by an officer of the rank of Major.

The numbers for ATC were massaged by a Burroughs 220, a room-sized machine equipped with 3/4 inch tapes as big around as a medium pizza. It ate punched cards by the gazillion and produced miles of printouts. It was the same machine that I had programmed at Stanford, which was the only thing that saved me.

Our most important system produced the Flying Training status reports, because the Command's single most expensive, critical, and quantified product was trainee pilots. These numbers went to the General Neil D. Van Sickle,[113] who was as no-nonsense as they came. We had botched an upgrade of this system, which prompted the General to ask when the hell that computer thing was going to start cranking out his numbers again. Because Van Sickle insisted on being briefed by specialists irrespective of rank, I got the job of telling him. And his staff. In the first formal briefing of my young life.

I shook, sweated and stammered my way through my talk and the General allowed as how he would be patient with us for a bit longer and it didn't look like I was going to be banished to Lower Armpit Air Force Base. I then approached my Colonel, hoping for a word of praise or at least solace. "Lieutenant," he said, with a pitying look, "join Toastmasters." Since he outranked me by five grade levels, I did.

I learned three things from that experience. First, know your stuff. In that I was lucky; I had four years of 220 programming under my belt.

Second, be prepared. I never sweated anything before or since the way I sweated that briefing. My Sergeant [114] and I went over every conceivable question, which was a good thing, because I think I was on my third sentence when General Van Sickle broke in and asked one.

Third, join Toastmasters. They're still around, and their system of peer evaluation of your talks remains the most effective way of becoming a good public speaker that I know of.

Know Your Audience

Back in the early 1970s, when the sexual revolution was in full swing and topless joints were springing up like mushrooms, I was dispatched by my boss to the Honeywell installation in Clearwater, Florida to take part in what promised to be a real headknocker of an interdivisional meeting. I had a couple of hours to kill between arrival at Tampa airport and the meeting, and had no interest in spending that time in enemy territory, so I decided to take the back roads around Tampa Bay to Clearwater. In the middle of what was then nowhere I drove by a double-wide mobile home that sported a Budweiser advertisement and a sign that read "Nekkid Wimmen." There, I thought to myself, was someone who knew their target audience and wasted no words in appealing to it.

While I certainly don't recommend sinking to quite that level, there's nothing wrong with tailoring your presentations to the way the people who can make change happen like to think. This is a balancing act. Basically what you are producing is an ethical infomercial, where the trick is to sell your results without selling your soul. On one side, you can blow the whole thing by not connecting with your audience.

On the other, you can degenerate into the worst kind of spin doctor.

As far as decision-makers go, there's an old military joke that officers can be divided into two classes as to intelligence, smart and stupid, and two classes as to personality, energetic and lazy. The ones who are smart and energetic you turn into staff officers, because they will never stop thinking and planning. The ones who are smart and lazy you make commanders, because they will be cool under pressure. You put the ones that were stupid and lazy down in the chain of command, because you can trust them to just sit there until they get an order. And the fourth group you drum out of the service.

Like a lot of dumb jokes, there's a grain of truth in it; many high ranking decision makers fall into the smart and lazy class, and surround themselves with smart and energetic types who do the spadework. Occasionally, and only occasionally, will you run into an enlightened monarch who does their own reading; the vast majority will hand it to some staff person.

There are two reasons for giving a presentation on your results: to get the staff advisors to read the report, or to get decision-makers to accept your recommendations without having read the report. If it's the first, you're in pretty good shape; if it's the second, you've got a big job on your hands.

If you are selling the report to staff types, then your presentation should be about the team, the process, and above all the sources: "this is why we know what we know." Try to pass out copies of the written report before the briefing. If the audience starts reading them instead of listening to you, then you've won.

If you anticipate opposition, which you should if your results are of any significance, then you should include what you've left out: rejected positions and the opportunity costs associated with them along with discredited factoids and the associated evidence. There are few better feelings than those you get from watching some potential critic slump back in their chair as you bring up and shoot down the objection they were going to make.

If you are selling the results directly to decision-makers, then you have a big briefing on your hands. You need to sell the report, present its conclusions, and justify those conclusions within the attention span of a typical audience. Many decision makers, especially the high ranking ones, are far from stupid. They read quickly, grasp concepts quickly, and get bored in a hurry. A useful trick is to start out fast and speed up until they ask you to slow down or stop and back up a slide. If you haven't done a lot of presentations to upper management types, you'll be surprised at how rapid a pace some of these people can take — often three to four slides a minute. Going that fast not only gets the audience's adrenaline up, it guarantees that there's time left for questions.

The absolute worst mistake in either situation is to pass out copies of your slides as handouts. I agree with the critics of PowerPoint[115] that a string of bulletized lists is a recipe for confusion and misunderstanding if not explained by a speaker. Pass out the report, or if that is not practical, make an executive summary as a handout. Include a discussion of the sources in it: what you believe and why, what you don't believe and why. If there is a major opportunity cost issue, such as not doing the obvious, treat it in detail. But never, ever let people walk out with copies of your slides.

Finally, don't be discouraged if your initial audiences are small. My project management class began as an internal Honeywell course, given by two of us. We'd go to some facility and give it to a dozen or so folks, and then in a few weeks get invited back and present to a packed room. I've also been on the other side, and watched briefers who were obviously discouraged at the size of the audience just phone it in. Don't be like that. Give every audience the full value for the time they grant you. You never know what ripples you'll cause in an organization, but you definitely want people to remember crests and not troughs.

Bullets to the Brain

You probably are going to have to prepare your own slides using PowerPoint or Keynote. The problem with these tools isn't that they make it impossible to do good work, it's that they make it easy to do bad.[116] People dive right into PowerPoint under the assumption it will help them organize their thoughts. It won't. It will capture organized thoughts, and even that only with difficulty, owing to its built-in structural limitations.

Trying to form concepts within PowerPoint is essentially working "outline first" with two further disadvantages. One is the brevity of the bulletized list, each element of which tends to have the intellectual content of a propaganda poster ("Us good. Them bad."). Worse, chopping a narrative up into individual slides destroys the flow and makes it easy to lose track; there's no obvious way to show that a main bullet on one slide is actually subordinate to a main bullet on a preceding one. I think these things are what lead critics to assert that PowerPoint makes people stupid.[117] It doesn't *make* them stupid, they already are; or at least victims of disorganized thinking. PowerPoint just doesn't help make them smart.

Getting the Word Out: Bullets to the Brain

You should be smart by this point in the process, because the preparation and writing of your report made you so. So your problem is now one of conveying that grasp of your material to a live audience.

On Stage

A lot of the problems with briefings come not from slide design, but from lousy public speakers. If you can catch and hold an audience's attention with nothing but your voice and your gestures, then it doesn't make any difference what's on the screen. And if you can't, then what's on the screen isn't going help much. If you have any doubts about your ability, join Toastmasters. And if you are free of doubts, join anyway; you probably don't really know how you come across to an audience.

The best use of slides is no use at all. The coolest presentation of a study is just two words long: "Any questions?" That happens when the audience has read the report before you start.

Otherwise, just walk in with your notes, say hello, and start talking. Watch your audience (the lights will be up), go into greater or lesser depth as you read their reactions and end on time. They'll think you're wonderful.

The second best kind of slides are pure pictures and diagrams. If you have storyboarded your captions as I described in the previous chapter, then show the pictures while you speak the captions. And rip through it — as soon as you see them start to really study a picture, go to the next one; a filmmaker I worked for at Stanford called this "cutting away from the audience."

Remind them that there's more in the report. Finally, if you have the budget and you have complex sequences of events to present, consider the use of digital automation, as was done for one study of the Deepwater Horizon disaster.[118]

If you're really sure that you absolutely have to use slides with words, put the section headings on individual slides, preferably with an illustration or cartoon. Leave off the bullets, just put up the words. Then treat those slides as illustrations, summarizing the contents of the section. Tell them anything, anything at all except the words on the slide. I say this because I am concerned for your immortal soul. Technological progress is universal, and a new circle of Hell has been established for people who read their slides aloud to the audience.

Somebody may ask a question. Don't answer it directly; instead, give them the page in the report or executive summary where the answer lies. If the question is significant and the answer isn't in the material, then you've got something to fix.

When I taught my project management course I was really tight on time, even with a two day schedule. I got the idea of handing out question slips and only accepting written questions. I collected the slips before each break and consolidated and summarized the questions before answering them. This eliminated repetition and prevented time being wasted by showoff questioners. I then saved the question slips and used them to locate problems in my prepared material. This trick is worth considering if the presentation of your findings is going to be closer to a class than a briefing. Tweets, SMS, and email will work just as well if, as happens more and more these days, the audience is on line while you're talking. The trick also helps you get questions from those who may be too shy to speak up in a group.

Finally, There's Always Marxism

The Brothers, not Karl. The exquisite comedic structure of their movies, like a lot of first-rate work, was no accident. Before they filmed, they took their shows on the road as stage plays, adjusting their plots and dialogue based on audience reaction.[119] The process I have described is report first, briefing second. If you're working alone, it's often more efficient to turn that around, and brief your material as many times as you can before you write it up. But please, think hard about what you are going to say *before* you sit down with your computer and open up PowerPoint or Keynote.

Afterword

I remember a lecture by Katagiri Roshi during which a student posed a long, involved theological question. Roshi peered at him for a moment and then said: "Those are interesting speculations, but the real question is, what are you going to do with your next breath?"

Intellectual speculation is a fine pastime, but it's action that makes the world a better place. There are plenty of problems out there. Pick one, find a skulk of foxes, and herd them to a solution.

Postscript

You're invited to send questions, corrections, observations, and rants to:

bitsmasherpress@gmail.com

and visit my site at:

www.bitsmasherpress.com

Once a week or so I'll summarize the inputs from readers I think are the most interesting and relevant and post them to the blog section of the site. Changes will be announced on Twitter. Follow @OldBitsmasher to keep up.

The site also contains links to all the Web pages referenced in this book.

Cheers,

Notes

1 Carlyle, Thomas. *Sartor Resartus*. London: Chapman and Hall, 1901. Orig. pub 1831. Available on Google Books.

2 Hartley, L.M. *The Go-Between*. London: Hamish Hamilton, 1953.

3 As quoted in Berlin, Isaiah, *The Hedgehog and the Fox: An Essay on Tolstoy's View of History*. London, 1953: Weidenfeld & Nicolson. The original is πόλλ' οἶδ' ἀλώπηξ, ἀλλ' ἐχῖνος ἓν μέγα

4 Berlin, *op. cit.*

5 Collins, James C. *Good to Great*. New York: HarperCollins, 2001.

6 Tetlock, Philip E. *Expert Political Judgement*. Princeton: Princeton University Press, 2005.

7 Tetlock, *op. cit.*

8 Rankin, H.D. *Archilocus of Paros*. Berkeley, University of California Press, 1977

9 Davenport, Guy. *Archilochos, Sappho, Alkman: three lyric poets of the seventh century B.C.* London: University of California Press, 1980.

10 Epping Forest Hedgehog Rescue, "Foxes are a major reason for the hedgehog decline"
http://www.thehedgehog.co.uk/foxes.htm
For a video of a fox pouncing on a hedgehog, see:
http://www.youtube.com/watch?v=nG80DcoscnM
Accessed May 2011.

11 Berlin, Isaiah, "The Hedgehog and the Fox Continued," *New York Review of Books*, October 9, 1980.
http://www.nybooks.com/articles/archives/1980/oct/09/the-hedgehog-and-the-fox-continued/
Accessed April 2011.

12 Bowra, C. M. "The Fox and the Hedgehog," *The Classical Quarterly*, Vol. 34, No. 1/2, Jan-Apr 1940.

13 Bowman, John S., Lieberson, Johnathan, and Morgenbesser, Sydney. "The Hedgehog and the Fox," *New York Review of Books,* September 25, 1980
http://www.nybooks.com/articles/archives/1980/sep/25/the-hedgehog-and-the-fox/
Accessed April 2011

14 Berlin, *The Hedgehog and the Fox: An Essay on Tolstoy's View of History. op. cit.*

15 Berlin, "The Hedgehog and the Fox Continued," *op. cit.*

16 *ibid.*

17 Suzuki, Shunryu. *Zen Mind, Beginner's Mind.* New York and Tokyo: Weatherhill, 1970. *Roshi* is an honorific given to Zen masters.

18   Conrad, Joseph. *Heart of Darkness: An Authoritative Text; Background and Sources; Criticism.* Robert Kimbrough, ed. New York: W.W. Norton & Co. 1988.

19 Hochschild, Adam. *King Leopold's Ghost.* Boston and New York: Mariner Books, 1999. Orig. pub. 1998.

20 National Center for Complementary and Alternative Medicine, National Institute of Health: "Mindfulness Meditation Is Associated With Structural Changes in the Brain"
http://nccam.nih.gov/research/results/spotlight/012311.htm
Accessed February 2011.

21 For more on Katagiri, see:
Katagiri, Dainin, *Returning to Silence.* Boston & London, Shambhala, 1988
and
Port, Dosho. *Keep Me In Your Heart A While: The Haunting Zen of Dainin Katagiri.* Somerville, MA, Wisdom Publications, 1988.

22 This is neither a book about Zen nor an advertisement for that particular path. Any Zen you might find here is just "cartoon Zen," a lazy way of illustrating points about doing studies. If you want to study Zen itself a good starting point is:
Aitken, Robert. *Taking the Path of Zen.* San Francisco: North Point Press, 1982.
Whatever form of spiritual activity you may choose, pick a tradition that has been around a while, avoid people who want to take your money, and do your homework before you sign up. The larger the ego of the teacher, the further away you should run. And don't believe anybody who tells you it's going to be easy.

23 Mumon Ekai and Yamada Kōun (trans.). *Gateless Gate.* Los Angeles: Center Publications, 1979. Like most Chinese Chan (Zen) masters, Mumon is known in the West by the Japanese version of his name; his true Chinese name is 無門慧開, in modern Pinyin transliteration Wumen Huikai, older Wade-Giles Wu-men Hui-k'ai.

24 Kozaczuk, Wladyslaw. *Enigma.* Frederick MD: University Publications of America, 1985.

25 Hodges, Andrew. *Alan Turing.* New York: Simon and Schuster, 1983. The author maintains a Web page at:
http://www.turing.org.uk/turing/
Accessed March 2011

26 Parrish, Thomas. *The Ultra Americans.* Briarcliff Manor, NY: Stein and Day, 1986.

27 Hodges, *op. cit.* Emphasis in the original. Gödel's theorems (there are actually two) deal with the limitations of systems of logic when you try to use them to draw important conclusions about themselves.

28 Zimmerman, Daniel. "E-Prime as a Revision Strategy"
http://www.ctlow.ca/E-Prime/zimmerman.html
Accessed February 2011.

29 Lakatos, Imre. *Proofs and Refutations.* Cambridge: Cambridge University Press, 1976.

30 Asimov, Isaac. "The Relativity of Wrong," originally published in *The Skeptical Inquirer* 14,1, Fall 1989.
http://chem.tufts.edu/AnswersInScience/RelativityofWrong.htm
Accessed April 2011.

31 Schulz, Kathryn, *Being Wrong.* New York: HarperCollins e-books, 2011.

32 Wood, Earnest. *Zen Dictionary.* New York: Penguin Books, 1977. This is a poetic way of saying that when you first contemplate a hard problem it looks like a big mountain. At the moment you solve it, it doesn't seem like a mountain, but afterwords you look back and say to yourself, "yeah, that was a mountain all right." It's a great feeling when you can do that.

33 Wood, *op. cit.*

34 Kahn, David. *The Codebreakers.* New York: The Macmillan Company, 1967.

35 Beckett, Samuel. *Worstward Ho.* New York: Grove Press, 1984.

36 Yardley, Herbert O. *The American Black Chamber.* New York: Blue Ribbon Books, 1931.

37 Tolstoy, Leon. *Anna Karenina.* Trans. Nathan Haskell Doyle. New York: Thomas Y. Crowell & Co., 1886. Available on Google Books.

38 Dōgen and Uchiyama, Kōshō, *Refining Your Life.* New York and Tokyo: Weatherhill, 1983.

39 Emerson, Ralph Waldo. "Self-Reliance," in *Essays: First Series.* Orig. Pub 1841. Available on the web at:
http://www.emersoncentral.com/essays1.htm
Accessed April 2011.

40 Nietzsche, Friedrich W. *Human, All Too Human: A Book for Free Spirits.* Trans. Marion Faber, and Stephen Lehmann. Lincoln: University of Nebraska Press, 1984

41 Jay, Anthony. *Management and Machiavelli.* Hoboken NJ: Pfieffer, 1994. Revised edition; orig. pub. 1967. A useful guide to a style many would consider manipulative; only to be used when nothing else works.

42   Brooks, Fred. *The Mythical Man-Month* (2nd Ed.) Boston: Addison-Wesley, 1995.

43 Early in my Honeywell career I heard this useful piece of advice: "Be careful how you treat people on the way up, because you're going to meet them all again on the way back down."

44 Ascribed to various politicians, and almost certainly apocryphal.

45 Adams, Scott. *Dilbert*.
http://www.dilbert.com
Accessed regularly since ca. 1998

46 Eisenhower, Dwight D. "'In Case of Failure' Message Drafted by General Dwight Eisenhower in Case the D-Day Invasion Failed, June 5, 1944."
http://www.archives.gov/education/lessons/d-day-message/
Accessed September 2010.

47   In the military, this is part of a doctrine called "Unity of Command." For a modern view, see:
Hope, Col. Ian. "Unity of Command in Afghanistan: a Forsaken Principle of War." Strategic Study Institute, U.S. Army War College, November 2008.
www.strategicstudiesinstitute.army.mil/pdffiles/pub889.pdf
Accessed July 2010.

48 Said to me in 1970 when he assigned me to manage a portion of the marketing and support activities for the Multics project. Renier finished his career as Chairman and CEO of Honeywell.

49 Anonymous. "Wiki." Wikipedia.
http://en.wikipedia.org/wiki/Wiki
Accessed January 2011.

50 As of early 2011.

51 I am indebted to the anonymous commenters to this Slashdot article:
http://it.slashdot.org/story/11/04/14/0336255/What-Is-the-Best-Way-To-Build-a-Virtual-Team
Accessed April 2011.

52 EDInformatics, "What is Voice over IP -- IP Telephony?"
http://www.edinformatics.com/internet/voice_over_IP.htm
Accessed April 2011

53 Publicare Marketing Communications GmbH, "Web Conferencing Sofware,"
http://www.webconferencing-test.com/en/webconference_home.html
Accessed April 2011.

54 As a starting point, see "List of collaborative software,"
http://en.wikipedia.org/wiki/List_of_collaborative_software
Accessed April 2011.

55 Housman, A.E. *The Collected Poems of A.E. Housman* (John Carter, ed.). New York: Henry Holt and Company, 1965.

56 For more on disaster recovery, see:
http://www.disasterrecovery.org/
Accessed March 2011

57 For details, see
http://www.nationalacademies.org/studyprocess/index.html
Accessed April 2011.

58 Bok, Sissela. *Secrets*. New York: Vintage Books, 1983.

59 *ibid.*, pp. 5-7.

60 If you are operating under formal security rules such as those imposed by the U.S. Government, the solution to your security problem is imposed on you, for better or worse. The only advice I can give you in such circumstances is to study the rules carefully and get to know your security officer well.

61 For years I thought this was the logic of Blaise Pascal's reasoning on the existence of God, the so-called "Pascal's Bet." Upon checking references, it turns out that I was not precisely correct — another example of why you should make sure you know why you know what you think you know.

62 For more information, see
http://honeynet.org/about
Accessed April 2011.

63 National Security Agency. *American Cryptology During The Cold War 1945-1989. Book IV*, pp. 402-405. Redacted and declassified version at:
www.governmentattic.org/4docs/
NSA_AmerCryptColdWarBk4_1999.pdf
Accessed March 2011.

64 Panda Security. "The Cyber-Crime Black Market: Uncovered"
http://press.pandasecurity.com/wp-content/uploads/2011/01/The-Cyber-Crime-Black-Market.pdf
Accessed March 2011. To be read with the care appropriate for a vendor document, but more responsible than most.

65 For further information, see
http://www.vpnc.org/
Accessed March 2011.

66 Eisenhower, Dwight D. "Remarks at the National Defense Executive Reserve Conference," November 14, 1957.
http://www.presidency.ucsb.edu/ws/?pid=10951
Accessed July 2010. Often misquoted as "A plan is nothing, planning is everything."

67 I joined the Air Force in June of 1962 and was commissioned in September, just in time for the Cuban Missile Crisis. I separated and joined Honeywell in 1966. During my time in uniform we experienced (besides the Missile Crisis) the assassination of President Kennedy and the start of the Vietnam War. Several of my mentors died in that, some in their third war. There was more to the 1960s than the advertising business.

68 For those not familiar with the military, the Air Force commissioned officer grades are Second Lieutenant, First Lieutenant, Captain, Major, Lieutenant Colonel, Colonel, Brigadier General, Major General, and Lieutenant General. In 1962 a Colonel wielded authority equal to at least a Brigadier General today. Nominally outranked by the officers were the Sergeants, whose effective powers were such that their cooperation in any task was essential.

69 Niwot Ridge Consulting. "A Gentle Introduction to Earned Value Management Systems." Version of June 2009.
www.niwotridge.com/PDFs/EVMSCookies.PDF
Accessed January 2011.

70 http://www.agilealliance.org/
Accessed February 2011.

71 As quoted with reference in Shapiro, Fred R., *The Yale Book of Quotations*. New Haven: Yale University Press, 2006.

72 Simon, Herbert A. "Rational Choice and the Structure of Environment," *Psychological Review* Vol 63, No. 2, 129–138. (1956)

73 Eisenhower, "Remarks," *op. cit.*

74 Jowett, B. (trans.) *The Dialogues of Plato*. New York: Oxford University Press, 1892. Available on Google Books

75 Adams, Sam. *War of Numbers*. South Royalton, VT: Steerforth Press, 1994. If you read only one book on intelligence analysis, this should be it.

76 Morel, E. D. *The Black Man's Burden*. New York: B. W. Heubsch, 1920.
Available on Google Books.

77 Mackay, Charles. *Memoirs of Extraordinary Popular Delusions and the Madness of Crowds*. New York: Farrar Straus and Giroux, N.D. Reprint of the 1852 edition.

78 Bok, Sissela. *Lying*. New York: Vintage Books, 1979

79 Theodore Sturgeon (1918-1985) was a science fiction writer who defended science fiction by noting that the percentage of bad work in it was no worse than in other fields, the "everything" in the "Law."

80 For example, you can learn much about the Deepwater Horizon disaster at
http://gcaptain.com/forum/offshore/4805-deepwater-horizon-transocean-oil-rig-fire.html

81   General Accounting Office, "Role of FAA's Modernization Program in Reducing Delays and Congestion"
www.gao.gov/new.items/d01725t.pdf
Accessed February 2011.

82 For example, see:
http://tagcrowd.com/
Accessed January 2011.

83 Madrigal, Alexis, "The (Shy) Woman Whose Words Accidentally Became Martin Luther King's"
http://www.theatlantic.com/technology/archive/2011/05/the-shy-woman-whose-words-accidentally-became-martin-luther-kings/238309/
Accessed April 2011.

84 Pariser, Eli, *The Filter Bubble*. New York: The Penguin Press, 2011.

85   Turing, Alan. "The Chemical Basis of Morphogenesis," *Philosophical Transactions of the Royal Society*. B 237 (1952). Quoted in Hodges, *op. cit.*

86 Box, George E. P. "Robustness in the Strategy of Scientific Model Building." Mathematics Research Center, University of Wisconsin-Madison, May 1979. Available from the Defense Technical Information Center, Accession Number ADA070213.

87 Odlyzko, Andrew. *Collective hallucinations and inefficient markets: The British Railway Mania of the 1840s*. Version of Jan. 2010.
www.dtc.umn.edu/~odlyzko/doc/hallucinations.pdf
Accessed September 2010.

88 Hoyne, Thomas Temple. *Speculation*. Chicago: Economic Feature Service, 1922. Available on Google Books.

89 Taleb, Naseem. *The Black Swan*. (2nd Ed.) New York: Random House, 2010.

90   Yudkowsky, Eliezer S. "An Intuitive Explanation of Bayes' Theorem."
http://yudkowsky.net/rational/bayes
Accessed January 2011

91 Doyle, A. Conan, "A Scandal in Bohemia." in *The Strand Magazine*, Vol II, London: George Newnes 1891. Given the early date of this story, I suspect this is a quote from Dr. Joseph Bell, on whom Doyle based the character of Sherlock Holmes.

92 Olivias, Rafael, "Decision Trees." http://www.lumenaut.com/download/decision_tree_primer_v5.pdf Accessed March 2011

93 The venerable 3x5 card is still a powerful intellectual tool. See Adams, Sam, *op. cit.*

94 Janis, Irving Lester, *Victims of Groupthink.* Boston: Houghton Mifflin, 1973.

95 Dickinson, Peter. *The Flight of Dragons.* New York: Harper and Row, 1979.

96 Known as a CONOPS in the military.

97 Seneca, Epistle 90. Quoted by Montaigne in the essay "On the Education of Children." A wide variety of translations exist; this is one of the most colloquial. The original is *Multum interest, utrum peccare ali quis nolit, an nesciat.*

98 For more details, see www.multicians.org Accessed 1995-2011

99 Saint-Exupéry, Antione de. *Wind, Sand and Stars.* Trans. L.Galantiere. New York: Reynal and Hitchcock, 1939. This was the motto of the Multics project. The original is *Il semble que la perfection soit atteinte non quand il n'y a plus rien à ajouter, mais quand il n'y a plus rien à retrancher.*

100 Adams, Sam. *op. cit.*

101 To see just how grim a business that was, see Masters, John, *The Road Past Mandalay*. London: Michael Joseph, 1962

102 Orwell, George. "Politics and the English Language." Orig. pub. 1946. In Honeywell marketing jargon, soothing abstractions were called "round sounds."
mla.stanford.edu/Politics_&_English_language.pdf
Accessed January 2011.

103 Strunk, William Jr., White, E.B., and Angell, Roger. *The Elements of Style*. Boston: Allyn and Bacon/Longman, 1999 (4th Ed.)

104 University of Chicago. *The Chicago Manual of Style Online*. 16th Edition, 2010.
http://www.chicagomanualofstyle.org/home.html
Accessed January 2011.

105 Capital Community College Foundation, "Diagramming Sentences."
http://grammar.ccc.commnet.edu/grammar/diagrams/diagrams.htm
Accessed May 2011.

106 Churchill, Winston. *My Early Life*. New York: Simon and Schuster, 1930.

107 Text available at
http://www.ntanet.net/KENNAN.html
Accessed January 2011.

108 Ogilvy, David. *Confessions of an Advertising Man*. London: Southbank Publishing, 2010. Orig pub. 1963. See especially Ch. VI, "How to Write Potent Copy." His advice was obsoleted by television, but has returned to relevance as the Web has brought text back to prominence.

109 For a short biography, see:
http://militaryhistory.about.com/od/airforce/p/lemay.htm
Accessed March 2011.

110 Possibly apocryphal. Various versions exist; this is the one prevalent at the time. More insight into LeMay's management style can be found by watching the movie *Twelve O'Clock High*, which was part of the curriculum at Air Force Officer Training School in 1962.

111 This was the Air Force motto at the time.

112 The actual numbers for 1964 were 3,021 pilots and navigators graduated, 115,873 students in classroom technical training, and 342, 249 classes given in the field. Staffing was 8,835 officers, 48,856 enlisted, and 20,005 civilians. Manning, et al. *History of Air Education and Training Command, 1942-2002.* Randolph Air Force Base, Headquarters, Air Education and Training Command, 2005. Available at openlibrary.org
Accessed January 2011.

113 Editor of the classic *Modern Airmanship.* (Princeton: Van Nostrand Co., 1959.) Now in its 8th Edition as *Van Sickle's Modern Airmanship.*

114 It is a military tradition that senior NCOs mentor junior officers. I was happy for all the help I could get. Sergeant Mezydlo knew how the Air Force worked, I knew how the Burroughs 220 worked, and between the two of us there was very little we could not accomplish.

115 Tufte, Edward. "Powerpoint is Evil." *Wired*, Sept. 2003.
http://www.wired.com/wired/archive/11.09/ppt2.html.
Accessed January 2011.

116 Norman, Don. "In Defense of PowerPoint."
http://www.jnd.org/dn.mss/in_defense_of_powerp.html
Accessed January 2011.

117 Hammes, T.X. "Dumb-dumb Bullets." *Armed Forces Journal*, July 2009.
http://armedforcesjournal.com/2009/07/4061641/
Accessed December 2010. The title is a pun on "dum dum" rounds, a form of munition banned by the Geneva Convention.

118 National Commission on the BP Deepwater Horizon Oil Spill and Offshore Drilling, "Chief Counsel's Report (Released 02/17/2011)"
http://www.oilspillcommission.gov/chief-counsels-report
Accessed February 2011

119 Gehring, Wes D. *The Marx Brothers.* Westport, CT: Greenwood Press, 1987.

www.ingramcontent.com/pod-product-compliance
Lightning Source LLC
Chambersburg PA
CBHW060038040426
42331CB00032B/1023